When we handed over the leadership of Life Church to Carl and Angela after our three-year transition period, Jill and I had a number of hopes and desires for Carl and Angela and the church. One of them was that they would build on the foundation we had laid to achieve more than we ever could for the ensuing generations.

*Pressing Reset* represents a major step forward in this being fulfilled.

Having walked with Carl and Angela through the past seven years with them as senior leaders, I can say without reservation that this book is not theory and is more than mere words on a page. *Pressing Reset* has emerged out of a work the Holy Spirit is doing in their lives. Their journey in leading and seeing Life Church grow under their leadership and example is a continuing joy to observe.

The messages this book is based on were birthed out of revelation and experience, lived out in relationship with Jesus, delivered from and with conviction, and presented out of obedience.

I know you will be challenged and inspired as you read *Pressing Reset*. Take your time over each chapter to ponder, meditate, and allow the Holy Spirit access to your heart and mind, to prepare you for your next steps in your life-long faith journey.

*Paul Bennetts*
*Founding Pastor, Life Church*


I have had the privilege of knowing Carl and Angela Crocker for a few years and have enjoyed their friendship and kingdom connection.

As I read this book, I found myself feeling I was in a room with Carl and Angela sharing our combined desire to see the church of Jesus rise up and be all God is calling it to be.

Like them, I am deeply burdened and convicted to see the great commandment and the great commission become the priority of the church, as I believe this is God's purpose for His Bride.

As we have seen much shaking in the church over the last few years, it is my deep conviction that God shakes to heal not to hurt. The shaking is for the making.

Each chapter of this book brings us back to God's original pattern for His church.

My prayer is that as you read this book, you will be readjusted and repositioned to get on board with God's now word for the church.

A timely word at the right time.

*Danny Guglielmucci*
*Founder, Edge Church International*
*Adelaide, Australia*

Carl and Angela Crocker are great friends, and diligent, wise leaders, who are led by the Holy Spirit. There is great wisdom in these pages, real humility, and vulnerability, which is what makes Carl and Angela such great leaders. I was inspired by how they seek the Lord, love His Word, and have led their church through extremely difficult times, to thrive and flourish and be a bright beacon light in our city.

I highly commend this book as one that will deepen your faith and inspire you to trust Jesus more as you grow in your discipleship.

*Dave MacGregor*
*Senior Pastor, Grace Vineyard Church*
*National Director, Vineyard Churches of Aotearoa New Zealand*

# pressing reset

# pressing reset

Recentring your faith and church on what really matters

Carl & Angela Crocker

Pressing Reset
Published by La Vida Trust
www.lifechurch.nz

With Castle Publishing Ltd
New Zealand

© 2023 Carl & Angela Crocker

ISBN 978-0-473-66716-0 (Softcover)
ISBN 978-0-473-66717-7 (Epub)
ISBN 978-0-473-66718-4 (Kindle)

Production & Typesetting:
Andrew Killick
Castle Publishing Services
www.castlepublishing.co.nz

All Scripture quotations, unless otherwise indicated,
are taken from the Holy Bible, New International Version®, NIV®.
Copyright ©1973, 1978, 1984, 2011 by Biblica, Inc.™
Used by permission of Zondervan.
All rights reserved worldwide.

Scripture quotations marked (NLT)
are taken from the Holy Bible, New Living Translation,
Copyright © 1996, 2004, 2015 by Tyndale House Foundation.
Used by permission of Tyndale House Publishers, Inc.,
Carol Stream, Illinois 60188.
All rights reserved.

ALL RIGHTS RESERVED

No part of this publication may be reproduced,
stored in a retrieval system, or transmitted
in any form or by any means, electronic, mechanical,
photocopying, recording or otherwise,
without prior written permission from the authors.

# Foreword

Infused with honesty, transparency, and stories of God's grace, *Pressing Reset* is the description of a dynamic journey undertaken by Life Church, Christchurch, New Zealand. Founded by Pastors Paul and Jill Bennetts, leadership has now passed to Carl and Angela Crocker. Globally, it is estimated that only fifteen percent of church leadership transitions from one generation to the next are successful.

Life Church has fallen within that fifteen percent and the leadership transition is one of the most successful my wife Greta and I have observed in our extensive national and international travels. In *Pressing Reset*, Carl and Angela explain why, and record the remarkable leading of the Holy Spirit into a whole new season for the church and new leadership team. Their journey could well be a model for other churches facing leadership transition.

Failure to transition well to the next generation is a tragedy, exemplified by Hezekiah, one of the Godliest of Israel's ancient kings. Hezekiah saw national revival, an invading Assyrian army defeated, and was healed of a terminal illness, his life being extended by fifteen years. Three years after being healed, the king celebrated the birth of his son Manasseh. Twelve years later, Manasseh became king in place of his father, and became the most evil king that both Judah and Israel had seen. Hezekiah squandered the extra years given to him, and failed in his greatest task – to leave a righteous legacy.

The wise and careful passing of the baton of leadership from the Bennetts to the Crockers has avoided this grievous mistake. In fact, Carl and Angela have not only taken the baton, they are running with it and are building a team of leaders who are accompanying them. Why has this happened?

It is because they have obeyed the counsel of the Holy Spirit, and sought to honour Jesus and give him primacy in the church. They have also been candid about their failures and successes, and have esteemed and listened to those who have gone before them. This has attracted the favour of God in a major way. *Pressing Reset* reveals the step by step unfolding of a new season and vision for Life Church, and the consequent blessing because of the church's obedience to this heavenly vision. It describes keys that can be universally applied to existing churches and especially those in transition. I would therefore recommend it for anyone to read, particularly leaders.

*David Peters*
*Director, Spiritlife Ministries*
*Auckland, New Zealand*

# Contents

| | |
|---|---|
| Acknowledgements | 11 |
| Introduction | 13 |
| 1. Prepare the Way | 15 |
| 2. Prepare the Vision | 21 |
| 3. Prepare Ourselves | 31 |
| 4. Prepare the Order | 41 |
| 5. Prepare to be a Light in the Darkness | 53 |
| 6. Prepare with Hope | 61 |
| 7. Prepare with Faith | 67 |
| 8. Prepare with Love | 75 |
| 9. Prepare to Go Fishing | 83 |
| 10. Stand Against Giants | 93 |
| 11. Stand Against Division | 103 |
| 12. Stand Against Inadequacy | 113 |
| 13. Engage with the Holy Spirit | 123 |
| 14. Engage Our Primary Identity | 133 |
| 15. Engage in the Right Fight | 139 |
| 16. Engage Your Air Support | 149 |
| 17. Engage the Comforter | 159 |
| 18. Engage the Gifts | 169 |
| 19. Engage in Good News | 179 |
| 20. Engage in Spiritual Maturity | 189 |
| Conclusion | 199 |
| About the Authors | 202 |

# Acknowledgements

To Paul and Jill Bennetts. Life Church's founders and our pastors and spiritual parents – without your faithfulness and obedience to God, we wouldn't be where we are today, and this book would never have been written!

To our staff, who willingly went on the journey with us and have continued to be obedient to God, putting Christ at the centre of their roles and ministries. We are grateful to you and your families.

To our editors and proofreaders who devoted hours to whipping our writing into shape – with special thanks to Brian Cowley.

To our Life Church family, for whom we are incredibly grateful and privileged to serve. Thank you for trusting us on this journey.

To our children, Caleb and Elise, who continually reveal God's heart for his children to us through you. We are so thankful for you both (and for the endless sermon illustrations you supply)! We love you.

# Introduction

This book is a culmination of three series that we took our church through over a period of more than two years. It has been formational in shifting us from where we started leading. In the beginning, our main priority was to make sure we didn't fail the previous generation of leaders. As a consequence, we became Sunday-focused, programme-driven, and somewhat people-pleasing. But, over the last few years we have seen a shift. More and more of our next generation are pursuing God independently beyond just Sundays. Mess and all! Our story is one of choosing obedience over popularity and God's power over our performance. And because we are human, we will continue to write that story for the rest of our days.

Whether you follow this journey yourself, or you decide to take your church on a similar road... strap in, you're in for the ride of your life. If you feel like your faith or church is just going through the motions, get ready to strip everything back to the foundations and rebuild. Be prepared to be vulnerable and uncomfortable. Allow God to search you and to sift you. Give Him permission and access to the deepest and darkest parts of your heart and mind and trust Him. God is gentle and restorative, powerful and full of grace and peace.

Our heart's desire in writing this book is that you come to a place where Jesus is central in your life. And that you live empowered by the Holy Spirit who brings you to a place of fruitfulness for the Kingdom of God.

Chapter 1
# Prepare the Way

At the beginning of our 'Prepare' series Angela and I had been leading Life Church for around two and a half years. It had been a steep learning curve, but we were grateful that our transition into leadership was championed by our founding pastors Paul and Jill Bennetts. Paul and Jill had birthed and led Life Church incredibly for 29 years and it was with excitement, fear, and trepidation that we took the reins in 2016 following a three-year handover process. We just hoped that we wouldn't make a mess of it and cause half the church to leave!

On that day of being prayed in as Lead Pastors of Life Church, I found myself asking God, 'Where is my vision?' and, 'Why us?' As was my habit when seeking God, I found myself walking on the beach asking God those very questions and He spoke to me about two things.

1. 'Don't take your turn.'

This was very confusing at first... Don't take your turn? But it was my turn now... I've been serving for years and been through a lengthy transition process. I've been prayed in. It is my turn!

Thankfully, God brought revelation to that instruction. He had placed us in leadership to help raise and release the next generation. We were a conduit to God's plans for the next generation. It wasn't for us to take the limelight or fill the platform with our voices, but to train and equip and allow room for the next generation to take their place. Ok... we can do that!

2. 'I want you to plant churches and help struggling churches.'

Nope. Not the most obedient answer at first, I'll confess, but I was already intimidated and stretched at taking over this large congregation of people at Life Church who had been led incredibly by the founding pastors for three decades! I couldn't even think about planting churches or helping others.

However, I made God a promise – 'I'm putting this on the shelf, Lord, but if you bring it up again with me or make opportunities obvious, I will be obedient.' You've got to love conditional obedience!

I would regularly walk in Lincoln with my mentor and founding pastor Paul, and on these walks, we talked about the idea of planting in the Selwyn area. It was two years into leading, and there was an unshakeable sense of God's prompting. On one of these walks, I strongly felt the Lord say, 'here is where you plant'. So as promised, I obeyed, and over the coming months prepared to launch our first campus Life Church Selwyn and it was launched on the 9$^{th}$ of September 2018.

Fast forward to 2019 – the campus was growing, and things were 'going well'. From an outward perspective it seemed that our church was thriving and growing yet we couldn't deny a growing dissatisfaction in the status quo. Yes, things were going well... but were we really reaching the lost? Were people's lives being radically transformed and healed? Maybe here and there, but that didn't feel like living in the promises of God!

We were invited by Pastor Jonothan Fontanerossa of Edge Church in Adelaide to come over and spend a few days with their leadership team and another wonderful couple who are pastors in South Africa. A gathering of the tri-nations! The conversations we had in that time, the prophetic words we received, accompanied by the deepening connection with Jonothan and Rebecca, set us on a new trajectory. As we said goodbye, Jon quoted us a scripture from Luke 5 in relation to parking our boat for a season. And this passage of scripture began a journey for our church.

While on sabbatical, the Lord gently told us that we needed to bring order and that we needed to get ready. He was also very clear that we needed to put Jesus back in the centre of our lives, family and church.

We realised that as we had received this gift of time and space to process our issues with God (fears, insecurities, hurts, disappointments, grief, etc.); we also needed to take our staff on the same journey. We were aware that as a staff team, we could not lead the church anywhere that we were not prepared to go ourselves. In early 2019, we shared the vision with the staff and for the next several months we led our staff to 'clean and mend their nets' and also put Jesus back at the centre of their lives and ministries.

We felt God say that 2019 was an 'amnesty window' for the staff. It can be easy in staff or leadership roles within the church to hide brokenness, pain and sin for fear of losing face. The longer you go on burying these things, the harder it becomes to expose them in leadership and the greater the leverage the enemy has on your life.

We told our staff that there would be no punishment for honesty – nothing would disqualify them from their roles, but that it was time to allow God to bring anything and everything to the surface that was unhealthy. Get your deficiency and brokenness out on the table and let's deal with it, whatever it is. We made counselling available for our staff to work through any historical or current issues.

That week, I got a splinter in my finger when I was doing some work around the house. It was so tiny you could barely even see it was there. Apart from the initial 'ouch' it didn't bother me again. The problem was that as the days went on, that tiny, insignificant-seeming splinter that I could initially ignore, started to become infected. It became more and more painful until finally it popped out and the relief was instant. God reminded me that the splinter is like our sin – for a time we can ignore it and tell ourselves it will be fine, but it will continue to grow and fester until it is finally brought to the surface. We had a window of time to choose to get the splinter out ourselves and treat it... or it was going to come to the surface anyway and it wouldn't be pretty.

No pretending. No bluffing. No covering up. Just honesty. We all needed to invite God into our darkness and brokenness and ask God for revealed truth. The Lord spoke to me and said, 'not everyone will make it if they refuse to do the work.'

My wife Angela had a vision that God showed her in relation to my own brokenness that I had come through. She saw a picture of a broken arm bone – the bone had not been properly treated and had been left just to heal on its own, but that had caused the bone not to be perfectly aligned and while it was still functional, it had a weakness and was not operating fully in the way it should. Then God took that bone and re-broke it, setting it correctly so it would fully heal. The process of the re-breaking was painful – as painful as the original trauma, yet it was necessary for the bone to heal fully and correctly and be totally functional as it was designed. So it is with us – were we willing to put ourselves before the great healer and trust him to potentially re-break us so that He could put us back into the correct order?

We instated compulsory 'retreat' days for our staff once a month. We closed the office and asked all staff (whether pastoral or administrative) to spend the day seeking God, opening their lives up to Him afresh, allowing Him to sift them and reveal to them any areas that needed attention.

Through this amnesty period, several staff were able to share their brokenness or sin areas, receive counselling, prayer and help through their restoration and be set free.

The next major task was to evaluate our church, its programmes and ministries and ask the question, 'is Jesus at the centre?' We were able to correct the focus in some areas relatively easily, some things were just a slight bump back on track, but there was one area that was particularly painful.

Our church operates a youth trust which employs several people as youth workers and runs programmes for school-aged kids in our community. My wife Angela was the chairperson of the trust and had worked for the trust in various capacities over the past several years. As she had gone from administrator to manager to trustee and then chairperson, it was definitely 'her baby' and she felt a huge sense of responsibility to keep the trust going and the staff employed. This was a difficult job as it operated solely on community and government funding along with donations from the church.

Pressure mounted as funding became more and more difficult and certain funding streams were only available to community organisations that were not 'religious in practice'. Over time, while convincing herself that it was for the good of the community (and the youth workers were still great witnesses), the Jesus element visibly faded out of programmes and became merely good works. Funding was able to be accessed because the 'religious element' wasn't in the programmes.

Angela came to our leadership team meeting during this process and sobbed as she confessed that she had 'veiled Jesus' for the sake of money. She repeated the confession with the youth trust board of trustees, also in a flood of tears. She said she felt like Peter who had denied Christ or even Judas for selling out Jesus for money. It hadn't been intentional; it had been slow and subtle and all under the guise of 'good works', but ultimately our community youth outreach had lost its spiritual dimension. Trusting God for His provision had gone out the window and the pressure to provide had been taken on by Ange personally in her own human efforts. Still to this day, she finds it hard to talk about it without tears but continues to confess it so that we won't go down that road again.

Our community programmes have been and are continually being redefined to clearly amplify Jesus and a connection with the church. Our mission has been restated to clearly include the spiritual element and the fruit that is coming from those programmes and families has multiplied. God is so gracious, forgiving and faithful.

Now it was time to prepare the church.

Chapter 2
# Prepare the Vision

God had taken Life Church on a journey of expansion and had spoken to us about taking new territory which came to us through scripture from Joshua 17. In order to speak to where God was taking us as a church, I need to briefly recap where we have just been.

> *The people of Joseph replied, 'The hill country is not enough for us, and all the Canaanites who live in the plain have chariots fitted with iron, both those in Beth Shan and its settlements and those in the Valley of Jezreel.'*
>
> *But Joshua said to the tribes of Joseph – to Ephraim and Manasseh – 'You are numerous and very powerful. You will have not only one allotment but the forested hill country as well. Clear it, and its farthest limits will be yours; though the Canaanites have chariots fitted with iron and though they are strong, you can drive them out.'* (Joshua 17:16-18)

We felt God say that He had more territory for us to believe for... but that to clear the land and increase our territory, we would have an enemy to defeat and trees that would need clearing. The 'enemy' spoke of opposition to the plans God had given us and the 'clearing trees' spoke of hard work and personal cost to receive what God had in store for us.

Because we felt it was a word from God for us, we worked together towards the launch of our Selwyn Campus. It involved opposition and some difficulty but more than that, it required hard work and personal commitment from everyone to make that a reality. It has been amazing to see that campus grow and flourish.

But God did not say this far and no further. There is more for Life Church to believe for. There is more for every individual and family to believe for. And it's true for every other believer and church that may be encouraged by this journey. There is more!

And so, we began this new series called 'Prepare' with the sense that God wants to do more through us, and He wants us as a church and as individuals to get prepared for what is to come. In our minds, being 'prepared' was all about getting ready for increase and growth and all that fun, successful stuff! In reality, what He wanted to prepare was far deeper and far more important than we could have foreseen. The date of the launch of this series to the church was 16th February 2020.

I announced to the church, 'This is the word for 2020 for us as a church. It is to "prepare". Prepare our church and lives in order to really live on mission and to see more people come to know Christ.'

I felt that as a church, we were to continue to push for all God had for us – to break new ground, to push past small thinking and to dream big for the future.

It all sounded good but the question for us all was, 'were we ready for that?' Were we truly ready for all God has for us? To do what God had given as future vision (to perhaps plant another campus, to expand our global influence, bless our city and nation) we would need to prepare. In a big way!

Prepare was a series that simply put, was about getting every person to live a life where 'Christ is at the centre' of it.

In our passage in Joshua 17, Joseph had come to Joshua

unsatisfied with the allotment of land he had been given – but the 'more' he was looking for would take hard work to inherit. Hard work is required for the promise of God to be fully realised! We were not to be afraid of the hard work required to see the promises of God come to pass.

Let me take you back in time from Joshua 17 to Joshua 5 to a passage preceding the entering of the promised land.

*At that time the Lord said to Joshua, 'Make flint knives and circumcise the Israelites again. So Joshua made flint knives and circumcised the Israelites at Gibeath Haaraloth.'* (Joshua 5:2-3)

The special meaning of circumcision for the people of Israel is found in Genesis 17. The context is God's renewed covenant with Abraham moving away from just contract to covenant. God again promises land and offspring to Abraham.

There is a purpose for this, that God was asking of Joshua – all the military-aged men who had left Egypt who were circumcised had died, and a new generation of wilderness babies had been born and were now of military age but were not circumcised. In other words, it's time to reinstate the covenant with another generation before they enter the promised land that God had for them.

This was an up close and personal procedure – it was vulnerable, messy and painful – but necessary for God's new generation of people to establish covenant with God.

Now please be assured that this activity was not the vision God had given us for 2020!

We are under a new covenant called the messianic covenant – and Christ himself was the sacrifice and a sign of God's covenant for all peoples on the earth. Both Jew and gentile. God is a covenant-keeping God. He sealed His covenant with us with the blood of His son Jesus on the cross.

I say all of that to show a biblical pattern for what it takes to enter the promises of God for our future. It takes hard work. It takes overthrowing the enemy when he opposes us, and it takes genuinely living in covenant relationship with God. It takes living where Christ is the centre of my life, not just a small part of it. Where I have given my whole life to Him and everything I have is His. I call it being 'all in' in my relationship with Jesus. Jesus Christ must take the primary place in my life – where He has access to all that I have, to be used for his purposes. Where the expansion of His Kingdom is more important than my personal comfort. Where I can live a life of obedience over popularity. Where I'm not afraid to be asked for more – more money, more time – in fact, it's a joy to serve Christ with all I am.

When I'm serving Jesus through the church I can have joy, but if I fall into the trap where I'm serving the church and the church is most important and I've forgotten I'm serving because of my love of Christ, then I'm setting myself up for hurt and disappointment. The order is wrong. It must be Christ *through* the church. It must be Christ I'm serving and Christ I'm giving to *through* the church.

You see, Christ should be the centre of everything in our lives and in our church... we have to be aware that we don't build the church to be about us. About our brand, our popularity, our lights, our technology, our clever initiatives, our programmes, our opportunities, or perceived success.

We are called to build a church whose focus is Jesus – so that the name that is exalted is the name of Jesus. That we celebrate and honour Jesus above all else.

That posture, where Christ is the centre, impacts everything. It impacts our church, and it impacts our lives and ultimately if we get it right, it will impact many other lives wherever we go. The cause of Christ then becomes our cause.

If we don't live this way – if we live lives where Jesus is not the centre, where something else or someone else has taken His place, we will not be effective. If we are not careful, we will become church followers at best, and not Christ followers. Being a Christ follower will lead me to a gathering of God's people most weeks because we love to come together and celebrate our faith together and join our worship for Him... but church is not the goal in itself.

It is God's heart that we would be covenant people who put Christ first and live lives that reflect that covenant. Christ at the centre.

If we can do that as a group of people, we will receive the promises of God for our church and our lives. We will inherit the territory that God has called us to inherit.

And here we were, 2020, where I felt God say that this was a year of preparation – getting things in order – getting our lives and church in order. I felt that as a people we were not completely ready for what God had next for us – but that it was time to get ready.

What was ahead had a cost attached to it. It would take people being all in with Christ at the centre – it is not God's heart that people would stay put or stay complacent or move to comfort when there is a world to reach.

What I've found is that in most people's hearts is a desire to serve God and live on mission and make a difference, but there are many roadblocks to seeing that happen. Many obstacles and barriers for people to overcome. You hear the vision or a message on mission, or you hear the phrase, 'we are not a church that *does* mission, but we are a church *on* mission' and you count yourself out because you find it hard enough to get through a week and help yourself, let alone think of helping anyone else.

Let's take a look at our central passage for this series.

*One day as Jesus was standing by the Lake of Gennesaret, the people were crowding around him and listening to the word of God. He saw at the water's edge two boats, left there by the fishermen, who were washing their nets. He got into one of the boats, the one belonging to Simon, and asked him to put out a little from shore. Then He sat down and taught the people from the boat.*

*When He had finished speaking, He said to Simon, 'Put out into deep water, and let down the nets for a catch.'*

*Simon answered, 'Master, we've worked hard all night and haven't caught anything. But because you say so, I will let down the nets.'*

*When they had done so, they caught such a large number of fish that their nets began to break. So they signalled their partners in the other boat to come and help them, and they came and filled both boats so full that they began to sink.* (Luke 5:1-7)

There is a part of this scripture that I love and have read many times. It is where the disciples' obedience to Jesus means they make a large catch enough to fill many boats. It speaks of the overflow, the plenty, the more.

I see the many boats as more campuses and partnerships, and that when Jesus is in your boat incredible things happen and many lives are reached. That's exciting! That if we are obedient to the word of the Lord and follow his instruction, we will have great success in the mission.

But there was something significant that happened earlier in the passage:

*He saw at the water's edge two boats, left there by the fishermen, who were washing their nets.* (v2)

And here is the revelation that I felt in my heart for 'Prepare' – this is what I felt God showed me: *You have to park your boats and attend to your nets.*

If the nets are clean and mended and things are in order, then Jesus can get in your boat and you can be successful at the mission.

As someone who is passionate about people finding faith in Christ, my heart is that everyone would stay on the water and keep fishing and keep on mission and keep reaching people... but God is saying that people's nets are dirty. They have holes in their nets. Some have their boats in the water, but they haven't even lowered their nets because they are in such a state of disrepair. Others have parked their boats permanently because their nets are so full of holes that to fish seems absolutely hopeless.

So, I felt that for a season, we needed to park our boats and clean and mend our nets in three areas:

1. The church
2. Our families
3. Our personal lives.

Over the journey of several weeks, we were going to explore this series of 'Prepare' and expand the discussions into our midweek Life Groups. We were also going to believe that it would be a season where people would begin the journey of mending and cleaning their nets.

**Firstly, for the church**

Cleaning and mending nets for us will mean several things as a gathered church. Some of our roadblocks to achieving what God has placed in our future is busyness – being caught up doing the wrong things or even good things, but things that God has not asked us to do.

For example, as a church we had been hosting a large conference every year in March. This was not our conference; we were just hosts providing our building and supplying a large number of volunteers and all our staff to help make the conference happen. It was a good conference with a good message, and it had been a privilege to serve at it. However, it took a lot of our resources and time at a key part of the year and was essentially serving someone else's vision. We made a decision to step away from hosting and resourcing the conference. This was a really difficult decision because there was nothing bad about the conference or the church or leader that was running it. Their vision was right and was their specific call and mandate from God for their church. All our volunteers loved being part of it. But it was a case of being obedient rather than just doing good things.

For us, this was cleaning our nets. A good thing, but not something that we felt God had led us to do. Something that our people loved being part of but was adding to the busyness of the church and not necessarily being obedient to the specific call that God was placing on us as a church for our city and nation.

Another example, and one that was harder to accept, was the parking of a new campus. We had felt so sure that God was leading us to the 'more', but with this scripture we knew we had to 'park our boat' of a new campus and trust God. We had already picked out the location and side of town we were going to go. Ange and I had gone there on our days off to pray, believing that it would be the site of our next 'boat'. However, God was telling us, for whatever reason, that we were not ready. Park the boat.

You'll remember in the previous chapter we talked about going through our church programmes and ministries to evaluate and adjust them to being Christ-centred. One of the core elements of discipleship was missing so we stepped up the focus on mentoring and discipleship and the training and equipping of people to live for Christ and be on mission.

In the next chapter, we are going to talk about what cleaning and mending your nets looks like in your family and personal lives. Cleaning nets is cleaning up the mess of our lives – mending nets is dealing with things that are really broken. If we will commit to the journey of cleaning and mending our nets, we will be prepared for all that God has in store for us.

I felt God say that there is a special grace for the preparation. People are dissatisfied with their brokenness and sinfulness and selfishness, and that it would be the Holy Spirit who would work on us if we would open our lives to Him.

We were to begin the journey of a life centred on Christ and to deal with our mess and brokenness, which restricts our effectiveness to live on mission. God is wanting the people of His church to live lives centred on Christ, where He is the most important person in their lives. We were to park our boats and clean and mend our nets – deal with that which is stopping us putting Christ first and living effectively on mission.

I am aware that so often we want to escape our burdens and yet I am equally aware, that though we want to run away from them, God wants access to them. From God's perspective, if He can get access and redeem our brokenness, He can use our pain and recovery to help others.

What we are disappointed in or frustrated by might just be a gift from God if we can break through in it. If we want to receive all God has for us, we must 'prepare' for what's in store. There is more for all of us and every one of us (me included) have areas in our lives to work on that, if left undealt with, will cause us to miss the mark or not live up to our complete potential.

**Prayer**
*God, we thank you that you are speaking to us – that you love us so much and have so much more ahead for us.*

*That you want to heal us and help us break free of the things that hinder us.*
*We choose Lord to open our hearts to you and say,*
*'Lord have your way in us'.*
*Help us and heal us and set us free. Holy Spirit, we ask you by your power to move in our lives afresh in this season – bring revelation into our hearts and minds. Information inspires us but revelation changes us, so we pray this would be more than information and would be revelation.*

*In Jesus' name we pray,*
*Amen.*

Chapter 3

# Prepare Ourselves

Get ready – bring order – step up and change.

Remember... according to Joshua 17, to receive the promises of God for our future it would require hard work. It would also require defeating an enemy who opposes us. There is an enemy who opposes you and opposes the truth.

Though parts of this chapter may feel confronting, God's heart is that we would each find freedom from the things in our lives that hold us back from all that He has for us. Sometimes we need to be confronted!

Let's look at our passage in Luke 5 again:

*One day as Jesus was standing by the Lake of Gennesaret, the people were crowding around him and listening to the word of God. He saw at the water's edge two boats, left there by the fishermen, who were washing their nets. He got into one of the boats, the one belonging to Simon, and asked him to put out a little from shore. Then He sat down and taught the people from the boat.* (Luke 5:1-3)

Verse 2 is the verse we felt God really highlight for us, that while Jesus was teaching, He was also looking and watching. He looked over and saw two boats parked on the shore and the fishermen washing their nets.

Out of this, God is saying, 'You need to park your boats and tend to your nets. Clean and mend your nets.'

You see, if we want to be effective at the mission of God to reach the world with the truth of who Jesus is, we must have our nets in order. To be effective on mission and to be involved in the cause of Christ in the world, we must each make sure that Jesus is the centre of our lives. Centre of our families and centre of our church.

My heart response to this revelation this year was, 'Surely Jesus is the centre of my life? Surely Jesus is the centre of my family and church?'

But the challenge lies in taking stock of our lives. Looking in our hearts and examining whether we have allowed something or someone else to be more important than Christ Himself.

Parking our boats to attend to the holes in our nets or to clean our nets is taking that opportunity to make sure that Jesus is at the centre of our lives. The words God spoke into my heart is that we need to 'unveil Jesus' to a world that desperately needs to know Him. That decision risks rejection and persecution.

We are meant to be a city on a hill that cannot be hidden. We are meant to be a light on a lampstand that gives light to the whole house. We are meant to be a witness for Christ in the world. But I felt in my heart that for many there is a sense we have hidden our light, or the power to the city on a hill has been turned off.

We have somewhat 'veiled Jesus' and there are numbers of reasons for that. Fear of rejection or persecution can cause us to veil Christ. Or perhaps we have listened to the voice of society that has told us that our faith should not be public but should remain private – so when we are out in the world, we 'veil Jesus' for the comfort of those around us.

I feel the heart of God is to 'unveil my Son. I sent Him into the world, for the world. Don't hide my Son away.'

When the church promotes its brand or its leaders or its platform or its vision as what's most important, we can unwittingly 'veil Christ' and people's attention ends up on the wrong things.

So, if we are going to live our lives where Christ is the centre of it all, we need to look at the many roadblocks that stop that becoming a reality in our lives.

Last chapter, we looked at the church. This chapter, we are going to look at our personal lives and our families.

**Let's start with your personal life**

What are the roadblocks for us personally to putting Christ at the centre? The reason this is important is because how I choose to live personally will affect my family and those around me.

In our culture, we learn very quickly how to wear masks (not the Covid type, the facade type) and pretend we are all good when in fact we are not.

We learn how we *should* look, what a fully devoted follower of Jesus looks like, how they act, and we begin going through the motions of what it looks like to be a Christian, but nothing is changing at a heart level. And when you are pretending, it is hard to put Christ at the centre of your life or to desire that for others.

We see that in the book of Samuel, where Samuel is tasked with anointing the next new king of Israel. When he arrives at the house of Jesse, he sees the older brother of David, named Eliab, and thinks 'this guy has the goods – he looks the part. Surely, he is the one!' But God says he is not the one. The Bible says, 'Man looks at the outward appearance but God looks at the heart'. This guy Eliab did not have a heart after God. But his younger brother David did, and David is the one God chooses. David wasn't even in the room at the time, David hadn't been presented with all the other sons as he had been discounted. David wasn't a star or a charismatic leader... he was a shepherd with a heart after God.

I felt God say, don't give me an Eliab church where it's all about the outward appearance. Give me a David church, a church that is after God's own heart.

And that's true for every person who follows Jesus. Don't become Eliab, where it all looks good... be like David, a man after God's own heart. Be a person who genuinely pursues and worships God, privately as well as publicly.

Then there are those who have major areas of brokenness and sinfulness in their lives that if left alone, leaves large holes and a lot of mess in our nets. If it is not attended to, it will render us ineffective in the mission of reaching people with the truth of who Jesus is.

The 'cleaning nets' is about dealing with the mess in our lives. The 'mending holes' talks about fixing brokenness. And I want to say this to you... If you will genuinely decide in your heart to do the journey and make changes, there is greater freedom on the other side. And numbers of our staff can attest to that. But you must personally choose to get your mess out on the table before the Lord and give him access to it.

Let me just name a few things that I think cause our nets to need attention:

- Impurity
- Insecurity
- Laziness
- Selfish ambition
- Ego
- Hidden sin
- Unresolved pain/hurt
- Unforgiveness
- Marriage problems
- Financial difficulties

- Entitlement
- Anger
- Addiction

This list could go on and on, right? But God is wanting you to stop living with such a mess. These things can be major roadblocks to putting Christ at the centre. To be effective and move into our future, we must go deeper, grow our faith and deal with our mess.

Well, how do I do that? It is your choice. You say yes to God first and foremost. You open your heart to Him and give Him access to your life through worship, Word and prayer. You get back to disciplines that are there to build your faith. You pray, you spend time talking to God and especially listening to God. You stop being afraid of what God might say and you embrace the truth. You spend time in repentance. It's not a common word heard as much these days, but repentance is being sorry for what you have done wrong and turning away from it. Lord, I'm sorry for my impurity – forgive me. Then move away from it – seek help and prayer and counselling if necessary.

Worship Him like never before. Worship helps me refocus on Him. It brings me close to Him and opens my heart to Him.

Read the Word – feed your life on truth, not just all the rubbish in articles and social media but with the truth of God's Word.

Take a half day or full day's annual leave and invest it into your relationship with God. We as a staff call these days 'retreat days' designed to retreat from the normal, the mundane and the busy and invest time into being with God – allowing God the room to speak into our lives.

Get to counselling with professionals if you need help to deal with some of your brokenness. Stop putting off the healing process.

Journey this season with others that you trust, so that you're not in isolation with your thoughts and emotions.

Bringing order into your life where things are out of order is so essential to getting Christ back at the centre. Here are some practical steps to take that help you to begin in this journey of Christ at the centre.

*Bringing order.* Use what you have currently for the purposes of God. Don't wait for the 'one day' when everything is sorted. Start bringing order now.

*Put Him first now.* Put Him first in your finance. For some of you, this is a step you need to take. To begin regularly giving to the church you belong to which Christ is the head of. I am amazed at how many people are still waiting and deciding if they should give to the church. You're not giving to the church! It's part of your worship that you are giving to Christ, through the church. You are giving *through* the church, not *to* the church – there is a big difference. One is worship and one is religious duty. God cannot be the centre of everything and somehow not have access to your finance. For some, mending nets is to get your giving sorted. Money is the god of this age, particularly in the western world, so no surprise the Bible references money and giving more than some of the more popular topics of grace or mercy!

Serving is another area. It's a way to practically put God first with your time. Use who you are to bless others. Again, not out of duty but because it's a joy to use our God-given gifts to serve the one who gave them.

But if you hear nothing else – hear this: pray, worship, read the Word – carve out time for the Lord.

> *But seek first His kingdom and His righteousness, and all these things will be given to you as well.* (Matthew 6:33)

The order here is important. Seek first His rule and reign – the establishment of His Kingdom and His righteousness and then all these things will be given to you as well. Your needs, your desires, your wants, in accordance with His will.

We would love the order to be the other way – God, give us all we need first and that would make it easier to seek your Kingdom and righteousness. You worship, you pray, you read the Word, you help others, you give, you serve – first! You prioritise the Kingdom of God first – the order matters.

I have a lot more to add to this point of mending and cleaning your nets personally. No doubt in the chapters to come, but the third point flows on from the last one.

### Our families

The reason it flows on from the last point is that the decisions I make in my personal life will affect those around me in my family the most. How I behave will influence and affect my family either positively or negatively.

God is a generational God... He thinks and acts generationally. One of the great blessings God has given us is family. That means He has given us great responsibility of influence over loved ones. Parents and grandparents influence kids – siblings influence each other. And many behaviours and beliefs are handed down from one generation to another.

God also puts us in a church family where our decisions also influence others – He gives us spiritual mums and dads or spiritual kids. He puts the generations together to help one another. To influence one another for the betterment of each other.

My decisions in my life have either generational blessing or generational brokenness attached to them. So, when we hear people say, 'it's my life and I can do what I want and I will live with the consequences', it's just not true. Your choices never just affect you – they have generational impact.

So as a parent, what I choose affects my kids, or it affects my wife.

It can affect my whole family and even affect my friendships. So, as you decide how you will approach this season of 'Prepare', just remember there are generational implications to your decisions. Who you are replicates itself in the next generation.

> *I am writing this not to shame you but to warn you as my dear children. Even if you had ten thousand guardians in Christ, you do not have many fathers, for in Christ Jesus I became your father through the gospel. Therefore, I urge you to imitate me.*
> (1 Corinthians 4:14-16)

Paul, in writing this, understood what it was to think generationally. But he was also confident that he had his life in order enough to say, 'imitate me'. Copy me. I wonder if we would be comfortable to say that with the example we lead. Would we be happy to say to another generation, 'imitate me'?

This generational impact thinking prompted us to launch a mentoring programme in which the four main areas were:

- Discipleship/faith journey
- Marriage and family
- Business and professional
- Finance

We realise that not all generational imparting of knowledge and wisdom needs to be age-related. It can also be experience-related. A younger person who has broken through in business could help an older person who is about to start out in business for example. One generation passing on not just their knowledge and experience, but their encouragement, support and prayer can make a huge difference to those receiving it. We strongly recommend people have a mentor in these areas of life.

The truth is, whether we like it or not, in families (both home and church) the next generation will imitate us. So that's why we must get our lives in order, because in doing so, we are making sure that we also clean and mend our nets in our families.

Let me give you a comment I have heard a few times over the years. 'The youth group is not really doing a good job of discipling my teenager.' Or 'the children's church is not teaching our kids enough about faith.' My heart response to that is always, 'you mean you leave the discipleship of your children up to someone else?' Please don't do that... Though these ministries are a part of teaching and growing, and we want them to execute that well, they cannot replace the family unit as the primary place for discipleship. The responsibility lies at home. People will move churches in hope of finding one that will do the job for them but it's their responsibility.

It's important for one generation to lead another generation to the feet of Jesus. But here is the stark truth – we can only lead and teach, train and equip from what we know and practise. And if we have holes in the net of our parenting, we have trouble because smaller fish can escape through smaller holes – hence the importance of cleaning and mending nets in our families.

I pass on what I think is important and I teach what I know. I teach my son to shave because I know how to shave. We teach our children to drive because we know how to drive. We teach them to clean themselves because we know hygiene is important. We teach them what's safe because we have learned what is safe. Why don't we teach them to pray, or read the Word, or worship God, or attend church regularly, or to give and serve?

Is it perhaps because we know many things, but somehow, we are concerned that they might see some hypocrisy in our lives? And even though that sounds tough, it's important to consider because we cannot look to someone else to teach the next generation. I personally must model what it means to be someone of faith. I am responsible to the next generation to show them the way of faith. To model a life centred on Christ. If I am not a good model, then the youth group or children's ministry must do it for me. If I don't prioritise the things of faith, then another generation that I have influence with won't either.

Now, by the grace of God, He intervenes in people's lives despite what they have seen or been taught. But we can be the answer to another generation if we will get things in order.

Bring your families to church – immerse them in corporate worship, pray, serve, give together.

In this season of park your boats and clean and mend your nets – we all have areas of our lives to attend to.

The flow-on effect of each of us being obedient to keeping Christ at the centre is that we would then see the promises of God and the increased effectiveness of His mission in our church, our personal lives and our families.

**Prayer**

*Lord, we turn our hearts over to you.*
*We give you access again to every part of who we are – the best bits and the not so great – and we simply say, Lord, have your way in us.*
*Prepare us, strengthen us and equip us with the courage to tend to the mess and brokenness and many roadblocks in our lives.*
*We thank you for Jesus and for the cross.*
*We pray you would renew in us a gratitude for all that you have done for us – that overwhelming sense of awe for who you are.*
*Holy Spirit, we invite you in these next few moments and in the coming days and months to have your way in our hearts and minds and lives.*

*In Jesus' name we pray,*
*Amen.*

Chapter 4

# Prepare the Order

The flow-on blessing of our personal commitment to Christ is that it would have generational impact and be transformational for another generation. I was confronted just last week with the impact generationally.

I picked up Caleb, my 12-year-old son, from school one day and was taking him to cricket practice. He just wasn't himself. I asked him if he was ok, and tears filled his eyes. He said he had a terrible day. He didn't like anyone, didn't want to be around anyone, everyone annoyed him. This was extremely out of character for Caleb who is a very loving and compassionate kid with a lot of friends. We got to the cricket field (Caleb is passionate about cricket) but he stood in the outfield with his arms folded and watched the cricket ball sail by him unmoving. 'Come on Caleb, chase the ball!' yelled his coach.

'No' he replied, still unmoving. I was floored.

After practice, back in the car, I asked him again, 'What is going on with you?' He said he felt angry and frustrated and didn't want to talk.

In that moment, I was tempted to minimise what was going on and tell him it's a new day tomorrow, have some downtime and you'll be ok. But I realised he was under spiritual attack.

Earlier in the week, he had been given the opportunity to play in a short-term cricket tournament that plays on a Sunday – we put the options to him and said if you really want to play then that's your choice. We put no pressure on him and told him that he could be a witness wherever he goes, but also if he played in the tournament, he wouldn't be able to come to church. Even though he desperately wanted to play in the tournament, with tears running down his face he said, 'I don't want to play cricket on a Sunday. I want to go to church.'

Even though it was a painful cost, he wanted to make a stand for his faith, even at the age of 12. I realised he was now under attack for making that stand. I needed to train my son, to pray with my son, to warfare for my son and to teach him that when you put Christ first, it doesn't always go easy. There's an enemy that doesn't like it when Christ's people put Him first and the enemy doesn't care if you're 42 or 12 years old. I recognised that my response to him could have generational impact. I had to choose between the easy option of thinking, 'it's just a phase, he'll get over it', or teaching a 12-year-old about what spiritual warfare was. I wanted to minimise what he felt, but instead I needed to teach him about the battle when putting Christ first. We talked it through, we prayed, he took some time by himself and he came through it, keeping his stand to come to church on Sundays instead of playing cricket.

Train your children, teach and equip them for what is ahead so that they might be a generation on mission but aware of the opposition that could come their way.

When I felt God speak to me about 'Prepare' and the idea of releasing this to the church, I knew it was going to require obedience to do so. You see, I want to preach blessing and faith; I want to preach the future vision and inspire people for the more I know God has. I knew this would be different for me, and it was also going to take the responsive obedience of God's people.

However, I have always understood the importance of

obedience over popularity. To do what God really asks of us will not always be popular, but popular does not release God's provision or blessing – obedience does.

That's why we were determined as church leaders not just to copy what was popular and what others were doing, or to import a process or programme, but to hear from God for our direction. That's not to say doing these things is wrong – it was just a conviction for us to do what God was asking us to do. To build according to the pattern God has given us to build from.

As part of this process, we decided to remove our Sunday night services for a season as we had felt that we needed to pursue Christ at the centre through prayer and to prioritise prayer gatherings and times of worship. Why? We felt that we had been having so many services to try and 'suit' people and that people didn't need more services or even more sermons for that matter, but in reality, we needed to become a people who understood the power of prayer. While attendance at these prayer services were less than the services we were previously running, we know with conviction that God was calling us back to 'my house shall be a house of prayer for all nations'.

So, we continue to press into these nights as is God's desire for us and to continue to pursue God's plans over our preferences. The challenge today is for us to acknowledge the power of prayer, whether it's a few or the whole church. This was a hard change because the services were great fun with a crowd. It felt like success to us. So, to remove it and add prayer meetings that would be less attended took a conviction to obedience over popularity.

We were on a journey to keep looking at everything we did that had become 'normal' and asking God to prepare us to be effective at helping His church keep Jesus front and centre, and to keep the cause of Christ on the earth as a priority in people's hearts. For many church leaders, success was beginning to be measured in how many services you had and how many seats were filled. This was a challenging decision at the time but now, having pursued this for a few years, I can hand on heart say it was the right decision. I love our prayer and worship times and know that the outcomes are the Lord's, not mine.

I am aware as we journey in our faith life, that if we are not careful, we can create a mindset that says I have to try harder and be better and I need to do more and give more and serve more. This is where the enemy tries to create a striving mentality. He tries to bring an 'I have to' attitude instead of an 'I want to'. 'I have to' means I need to try harder and in the end, it becomes a works-based faith where it's all about me. An 'I want to' comes from revelation received by the Holy Spirit and outworked in relationship with Him, not in one's own strength. An outward change comes from an inward transformation and fresh revelation.

The enemy would love to distort truth and oppose its work in your life to see you decide that you are solely responsible for your own mending of nets. But in actual fact, the Holy Spirit is the one who, given access to our lives, is well able to mend our nets and bring healing, forgiveness, transformation, renewal and a fresh worship and surrender into our lives.

Yes, we have a part in it. To recognise our need of God's work in our lives, to recognise and see where Christ perhaps is not centre and to say yes to God – yes, have access to my heart. We need to continue to position ourselves in a place where we can encounter God regularly, where the Holy Spirit can have His way in us.

That's why we continue to come back to the biblical pattern of worship, Word, prayer, family, community. It's the Holy Spirit's work in us that will bring order to the things in our lives and will purge us of anything that speaks of religious disorder, to bring us to relationship with Jesus.

When I pursue Jesus, I present myself to the Holy Spirit to bring order to my life.

Paul the Apostle, who is responsible for most of the New Testament, lived a seemingly perfect life as a Hebrew before meeting Jesus face-to-face. Paul said of himself, 'I had the law in order in my life – I was a Pharisee, my passion and zeal was persecuting the church.' His righteousness based on the law was faultless. It was attained through sheer will and human strength.

Then Paul had an encounter with Jesus one day while on the road to Damascus. This encounter changed his life forever. It's not knowing about Jesus that will change our lives, it's having personal encounters with Him that will change our lives.

Paul, through the order of the law, was gaining popularity and a name for himself – he was succeeding in the eyes of his peers. No doubt it felt good, and he revelled in the joy of his success.

Then he has an encounter and revelation of who Jesus is. Watch the turn-around in Paul's life as we read:

*But whatever were gains to me I now consider loss for the sake of Christ. What is more, I consider everything a loss because of the surpassing worth of knowing Christ Jesus my Lord, for whose sake I have lost all things. I consider them garbage, that I may gain Christ and be found in Him, not having a righteousness of my own that comes from the law, but that which is through faith in Christ – the righteousness that comes from God on the basis of faith. I want to know Christ – yes, to know the power of His resurrection and participation in His sufferings, becoming like Him in His death, and so, somehow, attaining to the resurrection from the dead.* (Philippians 3:7-11)

His life was transformed. Whatever were gains, he now counts as loss. His own striving to attain righteousness through his own human efforts are pointless, worthless, garbage even, that he might gain Christ.

It is righteousness gained through faith in Christ, not through human effort. His revelation is 'I want to know Christ'. In a relationship with Christ at the centre, my own human striving becomes of no value. It's through knowing Christ that the 'I have to' becomes 'I want to'.

You don't often hear 'I have to go on holiday', it's mostly 'I want to go on holiday'!

- I don't have to worship, I want to.
- I don't have to read the Word, I want to.
- I don't have to pray, I want to.
- I don't have to serve, I want to.
- I don't have to give, I want to.
- I don't have to attend church, I want to.
- I don't have to think generationally, I want to.

What was Paul's revelation? Not that I have to know Christ, but I want to.

I *want* Christ at the centre of my life, not I *have* to have Christ at the centre.

I *want* to 'unveil Jesus', not I *have* to unveil Jesus.

Are you hearing the difference? Paul wants to know experientially the power of Christ's resurrection. Not thinking only of the divine power that raised Christ from the dead, but the power of the resurrected Christ operating now in the believer's life. This power enables a believer to 'live a new life' because they have been raised with Christ.

Paul's encounter with Jesus changed everything but did not mean everything was perfect. Wouldn't you love it if the moment you accepted Christ into your life that everything came into order?

It doesn't! It's a journey for life. It's a constant desire and decision to keep Christ at the centre.

Paul continues in Philippians 3:12-14,

*Not that I have already obtained all this, or have already arrived at my goal, but I press on to take hold of that for which Christ Jesus took hold of me. Brothers and sisters, I do not consider myself yet to have taken hold of it. But one thing I do: Forgetting what is behind and straining toward what is ahead, I press on toward the goal to win the prize for which God has called me heavenward in Christ Jesus.*

I have learned that our continued growth and cleaning and mending nets is a constant decision to 'press on!' The enemy opposes the 'press on', he does not want believers who press on, he wants believers who get comfortable and rest in the already-achieved progress. He wants those who get comfortable with their growth to stagnate. He wants Christ-followers to live with disorder and disrepair.

I can't change the past choices or the past mistakes, the past apathy or the past indecision, the past restraints, or any of the past journey. But I can determine to 'press on' toward the goal to win the prize for which God has called me heavenward in Christ Jesus.

The enemy stands and opposes the 'press on'. He is holding roadblock signs in front of you like 'STOP'. Go back, it's too hard, take another road, it's too late for you, you've failed, you're a failure, this is not for you, it's uncomfortable this way, the accommodation here is only one star – it's five star if you stay put.

But the Lord is saying, 'press on'. The press on is worth it. The press on not only obtains breakthrough for you, it will lead others and influence another generation to also press on. All you need is found in me – so press on. In the press on, things begin to come into order – press on in worship, Word, prayer – press on by pressing into Jesus. You press on by pressing in. Not by striving!

You see, the enemy is intimidated by Christ followers and churches who bring Christ's order to everything. He doesn't like those who have determined to focus on the right things. One of the weapons of the enemy is his weapon of 'mass distraction' – if he cannot bring destruction, his next best move is distraction.

If he can get the people of God to simply focus on the wrong things or build for the wrong outcomes or strive in their own strength but have them believe it's all okay, he makes them much less effective.

That's why order is so important. That's why remaining focused is so important. That's why evaluating and tending to our nets is so important because in doing so we can get back to what's important in our lives.

Take the time to look and see if we have destruction, or simply distraction. I'm not convinced that distraction is any less derailing than destruction, to tell the truth. He will try to stop the 'press on' and disable Christ's centrality by distracting us with many other things (even seemingly good things) and is determined to mess up the order. Here is an order the enemy loves to break up:

1. Christ
2. Church
3. Community

That's a pretty important order. It's Christ first and everything I do flows from my relationship with Christ.

Then it's the church – the church is God's plan which Christ is the head of. It's the instrument for the expansion of God's Kingdom in the earth.

Then it's community transformation. Blessing the community

and changing lives. When this is out of order, we end up building with the wrong pattern.

If church is most important, then I am serving the church and I'm giving to the church and I'm building for my love for the church. Yet all of what I do cannot flow out of the church – it must flow out of me and my relationship with Jesus. If it doesn't, then I will end up burned out and disillusioned.

If community is first in the order, then I risk losing my connection of Christ and the church. I can end up only doing good works and lose my eternal perspective that Jesus is truly the need people have. I can also lose my connection to the church where I have my support network and a place for discipleship and growth.

Everything I do needs to flow firstly from my relationship with Jesus, through the church – both gathered and scattered, and into the community and beyond. For the mission to reach the world, all of it must flow from our deepening love for Jesus. It ensures that my service to others comes from a 'want to' heart and not a 'have to' heart.

*Whatever you do, work at it with all your heart, as working for the Lord, not for human masters, since you know that you will receive an inheritance from the Lord as a reward. It is the Lord Christ you are serving.* (Colossians 3:23-24)

We work hard at what we are doing: I am leading worship by serving Jesus with my worship gift. I am helping at kids' church by serving Jesus. I am loving a generation through youth working by serving Jesus. I am running a life group and loving God's people by serving Jesus.

The important order is – everything I do is for Christ. I give to Christ through the church because I want to give to Christ, not because I have to. The order matters and the enemy works hard at bringing disorder or distraction. Distractions are things we give our attention to more than we should and in the end take us off track from pressing on in our relationship with the Lord.

However, that's what 'Prepare' is about. Fixing holes in our nets, working through our brokenness and cleaning our nets – it's about bringing order and putting Christ first, so He is the centre of our lives. Holding firm to Him and pursuing Him, not just trying in our own strength, but opening our hearts to allow Him access and letting the person of the Holy Spirit transform our lives.

Now, I'm not a cricket coach. However, I have tried to infiltrate the ranks in Caleb's team and often give unsolicited advice. Particularly to Caleb, which hasn't always been welcomed. I'm passionate about cricket so I get a bit carried away on the sidelines and have a tendency to yell out my advice when I feel that Caleb could have offered a different shot or should have dived for a catch.

'Dad,' Caleb said, 'it's really important that you stop calling out from the sideline when I'm batting because it's distracting.' And I thought, 'fair enough, that would be distracting' so I committed to stop yelling out. But then I began just reacting physically. Throwing my hand to my forehead in disbelief, dropping my head and shaking it in disappointment, covering my eyes at a mistake. I'd be pacing, or demonstrating the correct shot... but not yelling out. Not making a sound in fact, because of course... that would be distracting.

One Saturday, he was batting and got caught out on 16 runs and, as he walked off the field, his posture just slumped. He was dragging his cricket bat behind him, his head drooping as he slowly walked back to the sideline. As he came closer to us, I could see tears running down his face. I could tell he wasn't happy, but I thought he wasn't happy with getting out. He turned to me and said, 'I didn't want my coach today, I wanted my Dad'. And that had a profound impact on my heart. I recognised in that moment the power in the weight of both my words and my actions to the next generation who are looking for love, acceptance, belonging, comfort, care and encouragement. When they fail, they need someone to pick them up and encourage them, not tell them they didn't live up to expectations.

I recognised in that moment that he was batting for the recognition of his Dad, not for the enjoyment of cricket.

There is a generation watching and looking to who is going to lead them. Who is going to encourage them and show them the way of love? Who is going to demonstrate Jesus and lead them to His feet? My generation has a responsibility not to be critical and judgmental of the next generation. Not to point out their flaws and failures but to champion them so that they will be a generation who takes their place and puts things in the right order – Christ, Church, Community and reach a world that desperately needs to know Jesus.

This season of 'Prepare' is for us, but it's not just for us. It's for the next generation. God is looking beyond us and through us to another generation who have a world opposed to the things of God, popularity to pursue and other gods that are easier to follow. But we need to point them to the one true God. It's never too late to prepare and get the order right, so that another generation might follow in our footsteps.

**Prayer**
*Lord, today we thank you for your ongoing work in our lives.*
*As we press on, we thank you that it's not about human effort,*
*it's about continuing to find you in the midst of our pursuit.*
*You, Lord, change our lives and transform our hearts and*
*redirect our desires.*
*We thank you today for your incredible grace during our failings*
*and your effortless patience to journey with us through transformation.*

*Pressing Reset*

*Thank you, Lord, that as we just keep saying yes to you with ever-increasing awareness you bring order into our lives.*
*And, Lord, this one thing we do: Forgetting what is behind and straining toward what is ahead, we press on toward the goal to win the prize for which God has called us heavenward in Christ Jesus.*

*In Jesus' name,*
*Amen.*

Chapter 5

# Prepare to be a Light in the Darkness

It was at this point in our 'Prepare' journey that Coronavirus swept the world and had its first impact on us in New Zealand. We were put into 'level 4' lockdown by the government which basically meant that other than accessing essential services such as supermarkets, chemists and healthcare, we were to stay in our homes and not interact with people to try to control and eradicate the spread of the virus.

This is not where we saw the series going... but as usual, God knew what was ahead of us and He had been preparing us for this season. Only several months before, we had employed someone in the specialist area of 'tech and media' to help us develop the ability to record and livestream services. And with the development of our new Selwyn campus and the camera and audio gear purchased for it, we had the ability to record worship services from our homes, edit them and view them 'live' together with our church family on Sunday mornings.

It also hit home to us that the 'Prepare' journey was as much about getting people to prepare their lives and faith to not rely on church gatherings but develop their personal relationship with God, as times were only going to get more stressful and challenging.

We reminded the church that while we were not able to be all together physically, we could be in one spirit and of one mind and therefore still have great unity across the body of Christ. We could in a sense still 'be together'.

As I reflected back on the beginning of this series, I could recognise the utmost importance of living lives centred on Christ. Nothing else can bring us the hope we need. Nothing else can give us the certainty of eternity other than Jesus. When everything in our world becomes uncertain, our God is never changing. Jesus Christ is truly an anchor for our souls.

Again, that's why His centrality is of such vital importance to us as believers. It is Christ that is our true north in our church, families and personal lives. You see, as much as 'Prepare' has been about getting things in order – there are things that God has prepared us for our whole lives. Things that God has readied His church for. That we would be a light that would shine in the darkness. That as things around us get darker, we realise we are prepared for such a time as this. We are prepared to carry hope to a world that desperately needs it.

You are ready for a pandemic. You are ready to respond to people who perhaps are afraid and uncertain – because you carry a true and certain hope that they need. As you watch the developing stories on the news and as you watch our politicians pass immoral bills, and as you see things declining morally around you – you are more perfectly positioned than ever to influence the world. To infect the world and infuse the world around you with great hope.

God has been preparing His church and continues to do so for times such as this – creating His people to be a city on a hill – a light on a lampstand that gives light to the whole household. As things around you get darker, the light of the gospel of Christ which gives eternal hope shines all the more.

It is no accident that you are alive on the earth at this time in history – you were born for such a time as this. Nothing takes God by surprise – He is sovereign and in control, He planned for you to be alive right now. If ever there was a time to be determined to be an influencer, it's now. Let your light shine before man that people may see your Father in heaven.

*You are the light of the world. A town built on a hill cannot be hidden. Neither do people light a lamp and put it under a bowl. Instead they put it on its stand, and it gives light to everyone in the house. In the same way, let your light shine before others, that they may see your good deeds and glorify your Father in heaven.* (Matthew 5:14-16)

We are the light the world needs right now – you are the person that others in your world need right now. Can I just say, this is the time for the church to run in its lane and spread hope and walk in faith.

There is lots of speculation out there, lots of uncertainty, lots of misinformation. A verse being quoted a lot is:

*For God has not given us a spirit of fear and timidity, but of power, love, and self-discipline.* (2 Timothy 1:7 NLT)

Somehow there began a teaching that if the church did not gather or people stayed home, they were giving in to fear and this scripture was being used as a reference point for that. This verse was given directly to Timothy by Paul the Apostle as a father would his son – Timothy had been raised by his mother and grandmother and it was believed he was a bit timid in nature.

Some people are naturally more timid than others. So, Paul is encouraging Timothy to operate in the power of the Holy Spirit – to function in love and to live self-disciplined.

Often this verse is quoted assuming people have already given in to fear or acted timidly in situations and therefore used from a negative framework – however, the intention of the verse is positive. To remind Timothy of the power he has received by the Holy Spirit that overcomes our human weaknesses.

We are reminded that we too in times of difficulty have the power of the Holy Spirit within us to love and to be self-disciplined and use wisdom that we might continue to be a light in the darkness. Using wisdom to protect oneself is not always timid or fear-based. God has given us an instinct of self-preservation that stops us from walking in front of a bus or stepping off a cliff. We are naturally meant to know what might hurt us – both naturally and spiritually (even relating to sin).

God has prepared His church to be a beacon of light in the midst of darkness. Hope bearers in a time of hopelessness.

*May the God of hope fill you with all joy and peace as you trust in Him, so that you may overflow with hope by the power of the Holy Spirit.* (Romans 15:13)

It's the power of the Holy Spirit that causes us to overflow with true biblical hope. That's why prayer and worship (as we have talked about through these 'Prepare' chapters) and reading the Word are such great disciplines. Because as we do those things, the God of all hope fills us again and again with joy and peace in the midst of everything, as we trust in Him.

We are not pretending to be full of joy and peace – we receive joy and peace and overflowing hope by the power of the Holy Spirit.

Hope is the forward-looking aspect of faith. Hope knows that regardless of what may come and go – or what may happen to us here on the earth, we have the promise of eternity where all pain and sickness will cease. Hope that reminds us that this life is temporary, but heaven is our destination.

Hope knows that God is faithful in His nature and is never

changing. God is with us regardless of what we face – He always has been and always will be.

*Know therefore that the LORD your God is God; he is the faithful God, keeping his covenant of love to a thousand generations of those who love him and keep his commandments.* (Deuteronomy 7:9)

*Praise the Lord, all you nations;*
*extol him, all you peoples.*
*For great is his love toward us,*
*and the faithfulness of the Lord endures forever.*
*Praise the Lord.* (Psalm 117)

God's faithfulness will endure forever – even in the midst of Covid 19, or the drop in the economy, or in the passing of new legislation that we don't like. In the midst of both plenty and loss, famine and feast – God's faithfulness will always remain and for that we remain always full of hope.

The Christian hope is hope in God, in Jesus Christ. It is the confident affirmation that God is faithful, that He will complete what He has begun. It is also, therefore, a confident expectation which waits patiently for God's purposes to be fulfilled.

There is a quote that goes:

*Life without Christ is a hopeless end, but life with Christ is an endless hope.*

What great hope we have in the gospel! Let us not be moved away from that hope. With Christ we have endless hope – that's why it is of such value to live our lives with Christ at the centre – because then hope is front and centre of our lives wherever we go. We have hope for the here and now!

God has promised that He is with us. If we were to ask an older generation to tell us of God's faithfulness, of His presence with them in the midst of situations, we would literally have thousands of stories of the goodness and faithfulness of God. And there will never be a time in our lives, regardless of circumstances, where there will be no stories of God's faithfulness. He is with us in the midst of it all.

In Luke 8, we see that during a storm that came up while Jesus and His disciples were out on the water in their boat, the disciples panicked, fearing for their lives. If a storm were threatening the boat I was in, I too would be concerned!

But they woke Jesus. I too would call on Jesus in that situation... and Jesus spoke to the wind and waves to be still and ordered calm. That instantly gave the disciples confidence. Who is this man who speaks to the storm and causes it to cease?

When Jesus is in your boat, even when we are unsure or uncertain, we can have absolute hope and faith in Him that everything will be alright. Jesus asked the disciples, 'where is your faith?' I can tell you this... after that situation, their faith was in Him. It may not have been before, but certainly was afterwards.

> *If only for this life we have hope in Christ, we are of all people most to be pitied. But Christ has indeed been raised from the dead, the firstfruits of those who have fallen asleep. For since death came through a man, the resurrection of the dead comes also through a man. For as in Adam all die, so in Christ all will be made alive.* (1 Corinthians 15:19-22)

We live with complete eternal hope. I recognise as you are reading this today there are many different responses to what is happening in the world around us – but for each of us, regardless of our response, we are all assured of the hope we have in Christ. And we are each prepared by God to spread that hope and to let our light shine in times of great darkness.

> *In the beginning was the Word, and the Word was with God, and the Word was God. He was with God in the beginning. Through Him all things were made; without Him nothing was made that has been made. In Him was life, and that life was the light of all mankind. The light shines in the darkness, and the darkness has not overcome it. (John 1:1-5)*

**Prayer**
*Father God, we are so grateful for Jesus.*
*We thank you that you have given us great hope for today and total certainty for tomorrow through your Son Jesus.*
*We continue to anchor our hope only to Christ and to not attach it to anything else.*
*Thank you that you promise to be with us throughout our lives in every situation.*
*And I pray that you would fill us with all joy and peace as we trust in you, that we might overflow with everlasting hope through the power of the Holy Spirit.*
*Thank you for your faithfulness throughout every generation.*
*Thank you that we have been prepared for such a time as this –*
*to let our light shine in the darkness. I ask that the Lord bless me and keep me, the Lord make His face shine on me and be gracious to me, the Lord turn His face toward me and give me peace.*

*In Jesus' name,*
*Amen.*

Chapter 6

# Prepare with Hope

'Prepare' has been both challenging and encouraging – and in many ways has been doing exactly what the name says! Getting you to prepare for times like the pandemic scenario. Living lives where Christ is at the centre of our church, our families and our personal lives.

The focus of this season has been to get things in order and our passage for that has been Luke 5:1-7.

As we were all in lockdown across our nation, and things were a bit uncertain around us, I was reminded of why this season of 'Prepare' was so important. As a follower of Christ, when I have Christ at the centre, I have the secure knowledge that God is with me through everything I face. My eternity is anchored completely to Christ which gives me security in eternity. Nothing and no one else can bring me that level of certainty, and because of that truth and revelation, I always have great hope.

Therefore, I am prepared for whatever is to come. I have my priorities in order. I have a correct value system of what really matters. I can live and love more fully because Christ is central, therefore He is working through my life. If Christ is centre, then hope is also front and centre in my life.

I believe hope is one of the threads God uses to mend the holes we have in our nets.

If holes represent brokenness, hurts, disappointments, mistakes we have made, unforgiveness (and a whole lot of other things), then hope is a thread that God uses to weave and mend our nets. If Christ gives us hope through His death and resurrection, then His death and resurrection makes all the difference for us as believers.

> *Surely He took up our pain*
> *and bore our suffering,*
> *yet we considered Him punished by God,*
> *stricken by Him, and afflicted.*
> *But He was pierced for our transgressions,*
> *He was crushed for our iniquities;*
> *the punishment that brought us peace was on Him,*
> *and by His wounds we are healed.*
> *We all, like sheep, have gone astray,*
> *each of us has turned to our own way;*
> *and the Lord has laid on Him*
> *the iniquity of us all.* (Isaiah 53:4-6)

Jesus paid the price that none of us could ever pay. He paid for our mistakes and our mess and because of what Jesus did we have unending hope. And the hope we carry, in what Jesus has done, continues to weave together and heal our brokenness.

For a lot of people, the healing or the mending of holes in our nets begins when we allow Jesus access to these parts of our lives that are broken. Many people carry their brokenness thinking, 'it's my fault I'm in this mess in the first place – therefore I deserve the state my life is in'. But if we each got what we actually deserve, we would all be in serious trouble.

In truth, that is what God's grace is – it's undeserved favour. God through Christ has paid the price for our mess and mistakes – that's the miracle of salvation. We get what we *don't* deserve. Christ died that we might be forgiven for the mess of our lives, and we receive His righteousness in return. So, we have great hope in Christ because we get what we *don't* deserve.

And when we fully understand that truth and hope rises in our hearts and lives, we begin to see the mess and brokenness in our lives being mended and healed. I want to try and illustrate this hope and how it works.

Brokenness and difficulty, and carrying mess in our lives, means we are living with a burden that at times can be too much for us to bear. We are not designed to be burden bearers but hope carriers. Burden wears us out, but hope energises and strengthens us.

Jesus says so in Matthew 11:28-30:

*Come to me, all you who are weary and burdened, and I will give you rest. Take my yoke upon you and learn from me, for I am gentle and humble in heart, and you will find rest for your souls. For my yoke is easy and my burden is light.*

Jesus gives an invitation to those who are 'weary and burdened' to come to Him! Our hope and freedom are found only in a relationship with Jesus. Our breakthroughs lie in Christ. Our genuine freedom is found in Him. Anything else we use to try to refresh ourselves or to carry our burdens are ineffective over the long term. They may help us avoid the feeling of weariness or burden for a time, but ultimately anything other than Jesus Himself will not last.

So, Jesus starts with 'come to me'. It's Jesus who ultimately gives us rest from the challenges that life throws at us. Take my yoke upon you. A yoke was a well-known term to farmers and workers. You would yoke animals together to pull heavy loads or plough tough ground. Jesus is saying, 'Take my yoke – be yoked with me. For I am gentle and humble in heart,' and then again Jesus says you will find rest for your souls.

Incredible imagery! Jesus is offering to do the heavy lifting when it comes to our lives. He finishes with, 'my yoke is easy and my burden is light'. Connection to Jesus means that our hope in Him is what does the heavy lifting when it comes to our burdens.

The hope you have in Christ is a thread that God uses to mend the holes in our nets.

Hope carries the burdens of difficult seasons. We still feel things, but we are not weighed down beyond the strength we have because of the hope we have in Christ. Many people are crippled by their burdens because their hopelessness exposes an inability to cope. But for those of us who have hope in Jesus we are given the ability to cope.

So again, I am reminded of the utmost importance of this continued 'prepare season'. God is preparing each of our lives, bringing order and even renewing hope in people's lives. We will emerge stronger and more ready to release the hope we have to a world that is so uncertain.

Reader, God knows exactly what He is doing. He is in control. God is not surprised, and God is able to use any situation to reveal Jesus to the world. So, can I just continue to encourage you to have time focusing on Jesus through worship, prayer and reading the Word. Encourage each other in your families to do the same.

**Prayer**
*Father God, thank you again for the hope we have in Jesus.*
*That because we have hope we are not weighed down beyond*
*what we can cope with.*
*In fact, because of hope, we have rest for our souls even in*
*the midst of difficulty.*
*Thank you, Holy Spirit, that you are with us in this season*
*of 'Prepare' – and we just continue to say yes to your work in our*
*hearts and lives.*

*We pray that even in difficult times and stressful scenarios,
you would work in our lives.
That these seasons would not be wasted, but you would use
these times to speak to each of us.
Lord, we love you today and continue to give you
all the praise you deserve.*

*In Jesus' name,
Amen.*

Chapter 7

# Prepare with Faith

In the last chapter, we talked about how God uses hope as a thread to mend our nets.

When we have the revelation of Jesus and hope begins to rise in our lives, we give Christ greater access to our pain and to our mess and He sets about healing our brokenness. We stop trying to carry our burdens in our own strength and Jesus carries those for us.

In this chapter, I want to move from 'hope does the heavy lifting', to 'faith gives us a firm footing'.

As much as hope is a thread that brings healing into our lives – faith is the substance in our lives that gives us a secure footing. When things around us are shaky or uncertain, faith is the foundation for us as believers that keeps us upright and secure in the midst of the shaking. Whereas others around us might be completely shaken by their circumstances, leading to feelings of insecurity.

As followers of Jesus, we will face uncertainty, but we are completely certain and secure in who God is and that He is with us. We know we are going to have flourishing seasons where everything is good and things are advancing, full of excitement, feeling on top of the world! And there will be other seasons of sticking at it, grinding it out, hanging in there – even when we are not feeling good about everything, when things are difficult.

If we don't live by faith in those seasons, we can end up

with holes in our nets, brokenness in our lives and doubt in the outcomes. Doubt can be a big hole in our net, but our faith can repair those holes of doubt.

Faith is essential. Faith keeps me consistent in my walk and response to God and how I relate to the people in my world, because faith is not based on feelings.

> *Faith shows the reality of what we hope for; it is the evidence of things we cannot see.* (Hebrews 11:1 NLT)

The world responds based on senses and emotions – how I feel about something. But faith takes us beyond our feelings; faith is totally confident in the reality of what we hope for. Eternity, peace in the midst of storms, overflowing joy regardless of circumstances – all that is promised in scripture. We can believe it because faith is based on the truth of God's Word and the promises God has given.

> *So, faith comes from hearing, that is, hearing the Good News about Christ.* (Romans 10:17 NLT)

Faith comes from the revelation of what we have gained in Christ and all that we hope for. It's faith that becomes our reality beyond feelings. Faith is not something we have every now and again. Faith is present and continuing. It's not just a virtue – it's a living thing – it's a way of life.

We are told here that faith is being confident or 'sure' of things hoped for. See, in our limited human understanding, there are realities that we have no material evidence for, but they are not less real because of that. Faith enables us to know they really exist. We have no certainty aside from faith and hope. Faith gives us certainty.

It is vital for all that the Christian life means and all that it hopes for. We have no material evidence for heaven, yet most of us reading this book know it's real. We have no material way of testing the immaterial things that we lay hold of by faith in God. It's by faith we gain our evidence of what we do not see. Faith stretches well beyond what we have learned from our earthly senses (that which we see, touch, hear, smell and feel). If we are solely reliant on our senses for how we respond to situations in life, we will have a pretty uncertain foundation or footing.

Our faith and confidence in who our God is and what He is able to do is the major thread to healing our brokenness and mending our nets. God is our certain footing in Christ, our complete security. God is able to do exceedingly abundantly more than we could ever ask, think or imagine.

> *Now all glory to God, who is able, through His mighty power at work within us, to accomplish infinitely more than we might ask or think. Glory to Him in the church and in Christ Jesus through all generations forever and ever! Amen.* (Ephesians 3:20-21 NLT)

Your faith in God goes well beyond how things seem or look in the circumstances of your life. God is able through His mighty work within us. That mighty work within us is to heal us, help us and transform us.

I think back to my own life growing up – I was a mess when I first came to church. Eventually I found faith in God through Christ. The Holy Spirit began to work powerfully in my life. I was an angry young man full of hatred for the world and everyone in it. I was suicidal, angry, abusing substances, completely lost, no clue what to do with my life. I was feeling abused and rejected by so many people in my life and living with massive bitterness from unforgiveness.

Over time and through a process of love, I was transformed completely. As my faith in who God is and what He was able to do in me increased, so did my transformation. My transformation became the evidence of my faith.

I have learned over many years that I cannot allow my feelings or even my limited understanding to determine the level of my faith. Our natural senses are not the basis for whether God exists or not. If we let what we see or feel determine our faith, we can get upset and angry with God when we don't feel or see Him at work, but our perspective is so limited. We can then end up with a wrong view of God and these misplaced disappointments can lead to large holes of mistrust and doubt in God's desire to help us.

Our faith is not in what God can or should do for us. If we limit our faith to that, then our faith is founded on anticipated outcomes. We don't have faith in outcomes – we have faith in who God is. What the Word says about God. My faith is not in what God does – my faith is in who God is.

My faith does mean that at times I will see circumstances change supernaturally with God's intervention. But my faith is not limited to the changing of circumstances – otherwise what happens when God doesn't change my circumstances? I have learned that God can and does change my circumstances as I pray – but at other times He does not change the circumstances but changes my perspective of the circumstances.

Let me illustrate how God showed me this in my life. At 26 years old I was having pain in my arms and struggling to work in my job. At that stage, I had started my own business in joinery. It was a physical job and I had pain doing it. I remember just being so frustrated with God – 'why are you not changing this situation, I just started my own business – how come you are not blessing me?'

I needed a healing.

I complained in every prayer about it. I eventually saw a

neurosurgeon who operated to remove one of the many lumps that were in my arms, legs and back. He diagnosed me with a condition called Neurofibromatosis.

My brain would grow benign tumours on the nerves all over my body and that was what was causing the pain. I had them also on the major nerves of my spine. The neurosurgeon's words to me were, 'I am amazed you're even walking.'

After that diagnosis, I remember feeling incredibly thankful that I still had my mobility to the level that I did. I remember this strong feeling of gratitude to God that I was able to still work and after treatment and surgery, able to live a normal life. My focus was now on thanksgiving and not on disappointment.

Our faith can change circumstances at times and lead to miracles, but it also changes what we focus on. That can be equally as important as a miracle.

God does not send the circumstances, but at times allows them. God can use them however He likes in order to grow and deepen my trust in Him. If you want to read of someone who had circumstances that tested his trust in God, but he did not give in, read the book of Job.

Since the pandemic, we are seeing massive uncertainty around jobs and are hearing constant doom and gloom messages about the economy. The world can only report on the facts that their natural senses allow them to. But people of faith are always full of hope – meaning we are aware of the threats to health and the economy, so we apply wisdom, and we abide by the process. We plan for a downturn in the economy as best we can. It's wise to look at our personal finances and see where we can maybe tidy up spending or adjust some habits to plan for a worst-case scenario. That's not a lack of faith – that is wise and a part of good stewardship. And I encourage everyone to do that where possible, if possible.

But faith in God means that we know God is with us in the

midst of all of it. He may or may not intervene in our physical circumstances, but we know He is in control regardless of what we see or feel. That's faith in God, not in an outcome – therefore we have peace in the midst of trying times and we still have joy. We still have a firm footing because Christ is our firm foundation.

I'm not trying to minimise the impact of job losses or financial hardship – because it is very real. But what I am saying is that our faith and our hope is in Christ, therefore although we might be shaken, we will not fall. We will always have praise and worship in our hearts because our faith is in God who is sovereign and in control, and not in our circumstances.

*May the God of hope fill you with all joy and peace as you trust in Him, so that you may overflow with hope by the power of the Holy Spirit.* (Romans 15:13)

You see, that's what faith does. It trusts in God regardless of the situation I find myself in and when my trust is anchored to God, I am filled with joy and peace. And when I'm filled with joy and peace, I overflow with hope.

My faith in who God is means I trust Him beyond what my senses are telling me. Then that thread of faith journeys me to the mending of my brokenness. As I read scripture, I am reminded again that challenges, hard times and suffering produce the best in people of faith. The way people of faith journey through difficulty releases genuine hope to others. 'How can you walk through that challenge and still smile, and still have such peace and certainty of it all being okay?' Your confidence comes through faith and not through your feelings or experiences.

My prayer is that no matter the season, we would never allow anything else to lead other than our faith. We would remain hungry in our pursuit of Jesus remembering that worry and concern would love to be front and centre in our lives, but the centre of our lives is reserved for Jesus. The one we have anchored our hope to, the one who we have found faith through – nothing else can take that place.

So, we keep Jesus at the centre through prayer and worship and Word. Remember faith comes by hearing and hearing by the Word of God. We are people who will praise and worship regardless of what we face, because our faith is in God and not in circumstances.

**Prayer**
*Father God, we thank you again for who you are.*
*In you we find overflowing hope, certain faith and complete love.*
*We choose today to trust you completely and not to doubt*
*that you Lord are in control of our lives and our outcomes.*
*The greatest outcome has already been promised –*
*that our eternity is secured.*
*We acknowledge that Jesus said, 'in this world you will have*
*trouble,' but He also said, 'but fear not for I have overcome*
*the world'.*
*So even in the midst of our difficulties we live as those*
*who have also overcome.*
*And I pray for us all and ask that the God of hope fill you with all*
*joy and peace as you trust in Him, so that you may overflow with*
*hope by the power of the Holy Spirit.*

*In Jesus' name,*
*Amen.*

Chapter 8

# Prepare with Love

As part of our 'Prepare' season, we have talked about hope and faith. And this chapter is appropriate to finish the trio and look at love.

- Hope does the heavy lifting when it comes to our burdens.
- Faith gives us a firm footing.
- Love wins!

Love has the final say.

Love has determined the end of the story. Love has secured eternity for us through Jesus' death and resurrection. Jesus said when he finally took his last breath, 'It is finished!' God's great act of love known through the truth of His sacrifice on the cross has won the victory.

Love is not an attribute of God, it describes who God is. Last chapter we spoke about how our faith was not in outcomes but in who God is and the Bible says God is love. The truth of the gospel reveals the God of love, through His willingness to sacrifice His own Son on the cross for our freedom.

> *And so we know and rely on the love God has for us. God is love. Whoever lives in love lives in God, and God in them.* (1 John 4:16)

As followers of Jesus, we know without doubt and rely on God's love for us. Our hope is anchored to Jesus, our faith is certain in who God is and love binds it all together.

*And now these three remain: faith, hope and love. But the greatest of these is love.* (1 Corinthians 13:13)

Hope and faith are reliant on our response to God. As we move towards Him, our faith and hope increase. But love does not rely on us at all. God loves us regardless of what we do or who we are. Love is God moving toward us.

God sent Jesus into the world because of the mess of humankind. Despite our inability to live our lives without sin and in the midst of humankind's faithlessness, He still sent Jesus. He did that because of His great love for us.

Our lack of hope or lack of faith does not diminish the impact of God's love for us. It only limits our revelation of God's love. But because of God's great love for us, we have faith and hope.

When I first came to church, as I mentioned in an earlier chapter, I came in incredibly broken. My birth father died of a brain tumour when I was 18 months old, and my mother remarried a man who was my father's close friend. The following years were very difficult as my stepfather was a heavy drinker and at times became abusive towards my mother and me and my siblings. Despite that, he had a soft side, and he always helped the underdog out, perhaps seeing himself in them. Over the years that he was in my life, while I so desperately wanted him to love and accept me, he never told me that he loved me. I never heard those words come out of his mouth.

I had no doubt that my mother loved me – but the lack of the love of a father had left a major hole in my life. It was a hole that I had tried to fill or fix with many other things. I felt like there was something wrong with me because I mustn't be loveable.

I had come to church with so much pain from the feeling of worthlessness that I wanted to end my life, and so end the pain. My motivation for returning to church each week was a pretty girl named Angela I had met – maybe she could fix the pain in my life.

Over a period of time of being welcomed to church and accepted by people, even with my mess, I finally encountered the love of God. I could tangibly feel God's love – something shifted in my heart and a light came on. A truth had been birthed in me that God was real and He loved me, and it began to well up in my life.

God's love opened the vault of my heart, and I accepted Jesus as my personal Lord and saviour. I remember saying to God, 'you can have my whole life', such was the impact on me when I realised what Jesus had done for me on the cross. Then my hope and faith began to grow. But it was love that won the victory; it literally conquered the death that surrounded my life.

Love mended the hole in my life that rejection had left. And every now and again when the hole of rejection opens up, it is the love of God that does the patchwork over and over again.

It was God's love that won my life. Because of the love of the Father sending His Son as a sacrifice, we now have direct access to God himself... direct, uninterrupted access to love. To God. That means we have access to mercy – the Bible says His mercies are new every morning.

We have access to peace. When there are storms around us, we can have peace in the midst of the storm. He gives us grace for every season regardless of what we face. God gives us all grace to face the circumstances we are in.

I was asked once, 'How do you survive leading in crisis?' My simple answer is 'God's grace'. God can grace us to not only survive in crisis but thrive. We can ask God for His grace because we have been given access to the God of all grace. We have access to supernatural strength when life requires more effort from us.

In our own strength we would burn out – but access to the God of love gives us the strength we need.

Because of the Father's great love for us discovered in Christ and at work in us through the Holy Spirit, we have all we need. That's why I can say with confidence that love wins.

We see this great prayer prayed by Paul the Apostle in the book of Ephesians:

> *For this reason, I kneel before the Father, from whom every family in heaven and on earth derives its name. I pray that out of His glorious riches He may strengthen you with power through his Spirit in your inner being, so that Christ may dwell in your hearts through faith. And I pray that you, being rooted and established in love, may have power, together with all the Lord's holy people, to grasp how wide and long and high and deep is the love of Christ, and to know this love that surpasses knowledge – that you may be filled to the measure of all the fullness of God.*
> (Ephesians 3:14-19)

Paul's prayer is based on his revelation of what we now have access to from the Father because of Jesus. He prays that out of God's glorious riches, God's provision of all that we need as children of God here on the earth, He may strengthen us all with power through His Spirit in our inner beings.

God loves you so much and because of His great love for you, there is access to all you need, and He deposits it in your life by the Holy Spirit. You can make it. You *will* make it. You have been given access to a loving father who has everything you need and because the Spirit dwells in you, Christ also dwells in your heart.

Therefore, hope is front and centre, and faith is evident. Your burdens are lifted by hope and your life is steady through faith – all held together in perfect love.

I don't know what your needs are, but God knows every need you have. Jesus' death and resurrection means that for those who have accepted Jesus into their lives as their personal Lord and Saviour, you have direct access to all that you need in God (note, I didn't say want...).

Paul goes on – *I pray that together with all God's people* (that's all of us included in this prayer) *we would be able to grasp how wide and long and deep is the love of Christ.*

As you pray, as you worship, as you read the Word and give thanks, I pray that the Spirit of God would help you to grasp just how much you are loved.

I want to finish this chapter with a hymn that has a powerful story attached to it. The hymn is entitled 'He giveth more grace'.

It's a hymn you will find in an old Salvation Army songbook. It was written by a woman named Annie Flint who was born in 1866. Annie was orphaned at age 6. She was then adopted into a Baptist family and at age 8 in a revival meeting she found faith in Christ. As Annie grew up, she was a positive person who always chose to look on the bright side of life – her faith gave her that disposition.

Annie trained to be a teacher but two years into teaching she was struck with the onset of arthritis. The arthritis got so bad eventually it became difficult for Annie to even walk. Some of her dreams were gone forever – she had dreamed of being a concert pianist but couldn't even play the piano anymore. Then her adoptive parents died only months apart from each other. She found herself orphaned for a second time in her life.

With very little money, she received news from her doctor that she would be confined to a wheelchair for life, and she was now facing this battle alone. It would be easy to say life had been unfair to Annie, but Annie had hope and faith in an all-loving God.

Because of that, Annie took the view that because of what she had walked through, she could write poems and hymns with real understanding. She believed that her writings from her place of suffering could bring comfort to thousands of others who faced difficulty. Annie did not waste her pain with disappointment... she used her pain by giving expression to her faith in Christ through song.

The verses she wrote gave her comfort during her long suffering. Annie's faith never faltered in who God was. She found hope in the truths of scripture that lifted her burdens and allowed her to express her faith.

Here are the words to Annie's hymn 'He giveth more grace':

*He giveth more grace when the burdens grow greater,*
*He sendeth more strength when the labors increase;*
*To added afflictions He addeth His mercy,*
*To multiplied trials, His multiplied peace.*
*When we have exhausted our store of endurance,*
*When our strength has failed ere the day is half done,*
*When we reach the end of our hoarded resources*
*Our Father's full giving is only begun.*
*Fear not that thy need shall exceed His provision,*
*Our God ever yearns His resources to share;*
*Lean hard on the arm everlasting, availing;*
*The Father both thee and thy load will upbear.*
*His love has no limits, His grace has no measure,*
*His power no boundary known unto men;*
*For out of His infinite riches in Jesus*
*He giveth, and giveth, and giveth again.*

**Prayer**
*Lord, we thank you for everything we have access to because of your incredible love for us all. With fresh gratitude we thank you for Jesus and all that was accomplished on the cross.*

*Prepare with Love*

*We thank you that your grace is greater than our burdens.*
*We thank you for strength and mercy and multiplied peace.*
*We thank you for endurance in seasons of hardship.*
*We thank you, Lord, for all that you give.*
*Your love has no limits, your grace has no measure,*
*your power no boundary and out of your riches, you giveth and*
*giveth and giveth again.*
*Lord, nothing else will do.*
*Nothing else can give us what we need in life other than the love of*
*God found in Christ Jesus. Lord, you are all we want.*
*So, Lord, again we open up our hearts to you.*
*Take each of us back to where it all started – it started with*
*the truth of who Jesus is and what Jesus did for us all through*
*His death and resurrection.*
*We thank you that hope does the heavy lifting when it comes to*
*our burdens, that faith gives us a firm footing and that ultimately,*
*love wins.*

*In Jesus' name,*
*Amen.*

Chapter 9
# Prepare to Go Fishing

I started this series reminding us that God had more ahead for us – more territory for us to receive and to believe Him for. The 'more territory' meant reaching more people with the gospel – we also believed He had more for every individual and family.

Our 'Prepare' series was designed by God to get us ready for the more He had. That the more externally was a result of the more internally. That God wanted more access to our hearts and lives to heal our brokenness and overcome the obstacles that perhaps were stopping us from living lives where Christ was at the centre.

Two thousand and twenty was to be a year to get our church and lives in order to really live on mission and to see more people afforded the opportunity to come to know Christ. I felt as a church we were to continue to push for all God has for us – to break new ground, to push past small thinking and to dream big for our future.

In order to achieve what God had given as vision, to perhaps plant another campus, to expand our global influence, bless our city and nation, we needed to prepare for it. Prepare was a series that simply put, was about getting every person to live a life where 'Christ is at the centre'. Where I have given my whole life to Him – everything I have is His. We call it being 'all in', in my relationship with Jesus. Where Jesus Christ takes the primary place in my life – where He has access to all that I have, to be used for His purposes. Where the expansion of His Kingdom is more important than my personal comfort. Where I can live a life of obedience over popularity. Where I'm not afraid to be asked for more. More money or more time – in fact, it's a joy to serve Christ with all I am.

The urgency I felt in my spirit was to build lives and a church whose focus is Jesus – that the name that is exalted here in this place is no other than the name of Jesus.

If we live lives where Jesus is not the centre, where something else or someone else has taken His place, we will lose our effectiveness and if we are not careful, we will become church followers rather than Christ followers. We were never designed to just be church goers but to be Christ followers.

In most people's hearts is a desire to serve God and live on mission and make a difference, but there are many roadblocks to seeing that happen. Many obstacles and barriers for people to overcome.

> *One day as Jesus was standing by the Lake of Gennesaret, the people were crowding around Him and listening to the word of God. He saw at the water's edge two boats, left there by the fishermen, who were washing their nets. He got into one of the boats, the one belonging to Simon, and asked him to put out a little from shore. Then He sat down and taught the people from the boat.*
>
> *When He had finished speaking, He said to Simon, 'Put out into deep water, and let down the nets for a catch.'*
>
> *Simon answered, 'Master, we've worked hard all night and haven't caught anything. But because you say so, I will let down the nets.'*
>
> *When they had done so, they caught such a large number of fish that their nets began to break. So they signalled their partners in the other boat to come and help them, and they came and filled both boats so full that they began to sink.* (Luke 5:1-7)

Much of this passage speaks to the more that happens when we are obedient to the word of the Lord. They received a massive catch – it's exciting, it's big, it's miraculous. As church leaders, that's appealing.

But what if we were ready to fish but our nets were broken and in disrepair. The catch might be there, but we would be ineffective in seeing many fish caught at all.

The verse that stood out was verse 2:

*He saw at the water's edge two boats, left there by the fishermen, who were washing their nets.*

Let me remind you, this is what I felt God revealed to me: 'You have to park your boats and clean and mend your nets.' If the nets (which represent our lives) are clean and mended and things are in order, then when Jesus gets in your boat, you can be successful at the mission.

I felt that for a season, to a degree, we needed to park our boats and clean and mend our nets in three areas:

1. The church
2. Our families
3. Our personal lives.

Well, we obviously had no idea that in fact 'Prepare' was going to precede a lockdown because of a global health crisis. In lockdown, I was reminded afresh of the value of the gathered church – its role in the expansion of God's Kingdom and that it's the distribution centre for the good news of Jesus.

I had time alone with my family and no one else – a chance to have conversations about what is truly of value when life is uncertain. And personally, time to reflect on where my hope is firmly anchored.

We were going to have our boats well and truly parked for us and this was not something we had seen coming. But the account in Luke shows us that if our nets are mended and clean, we are prepared for the large catch of fish that God has planned for us to receive.

The story shows us that when Jesus is centre of our lives and is in our boat, we are incredibly effective in our mission. That's why we want to worship – that lifts up Jesus. The Word that points us to Jesus and lives that point others to Him.

When the disciples fished in their own expertise and knowledge, they caught nothing, but the next morning when Jesus enters their world the fishing trip is miraculous. Off the back of that miracle, Jesus calls these men to follow Him and tells them He will make them into fishers of people.

You may remember in an earlier chapter that part of our 'Prepare' journey was to 'park the boat' of a new campus. At the time this was disappointing as we had a heart for a location, and it really felt like God's will when we had been out there praying. However, God said park it and we did.

As we are in our last chapter of the 'Prepare' journey – let me tell you what happened several months later. We received an email from a church leader that had a congregation in the side of town that we had been praying about planting in. He had sent out this email to ten church leaders explaining their journey as a church and asking if anyone felt a specific leading from God as to what they should do. Post-earthquake, they had built a new building, but their numbers were lessening and as pastors, they had served their congregation and community faithfully, but were ready to hand over.

I was reminded about the word God gave me right back at the start of our leadership – plant churches and help struggling churches. So, I replied to the email and offered to meet and discuss.

I made clear that we would be happy to help them, whatever their journey might be.

Over the next several weeks after meeting with the pastors and their leadership team, it was undeniable that there was a synergy of vision. God was in this. Making a long story short, these faithful and courageous pastors and their team transferred their church building, land and assets over to us to become a Life Church campus. Life Church QE2 was launched.

Amazing to think that we were pursuing a rented facility in this same side of town only several months ago. We felt disappointed that God had told us to 'park our boat' but we did not have the foresight He had to know what was coming! Now we had an incredible new facility with land that was mortgage free, an existing congregation that were nervous but excited for change and missional members of Life Church that were going to add to the family and be part of the plant. And if that wasn't enough... we received another miracle.

We had recently relocated and repurposed a kids' community building on our property at our central campus, La Vida. The construction company that had located that building for us made contact when they heard that we were starting a new project in the East. The conversation went something like this... 'Hi mate, we heard you're doing something over in New Brighton – if you are wanting a similar building to the one we've just done, we've got one that would be perfect. It's a set of classrooms that needs to be transported off a school site. We'd rather not transfer it twice, so we were wondering... do you want it for $1?'

$1??? We had already looked at this building online and seen that it was selling for $170k. Instead, God's provision meant we got it for $1 and just had to pay the costs of moving it and tailoring it to our needs. It was moved onto the new campus site within weeks. The vision we had so strongly aligned with the former pastors on was our heart to reach community youth, and we had a building provided that we were able to customise for that very purpose.

Pays to be obedient to God's instruction!

Going back to our text, let's fast forward to a parallel story to our Luke 5 text that happens three years later.

These men had been in Jesus' life and ministry for three years and had seen miracles happen, and in the end witnessed Jesus be captured, put through a trial and crucified. Peter had denied knowing Jesus. Three days later, Jesus rose from the dead and He appeared to His disciples three times. And I want us to look at one of these accounts in the Gospel of John.

> *Afterward Jesus appeared again to His disciples, by the Sea of Galilee. It happened this way: Simon Peter, Thomas (also known as Didymus), Nathanael from Cana in Galilee, the sons of Zebedee, and two other disciples were together. 'I'm going out to fish,' Simon Peter told them, and they said, 'We'll go with you.' So they went out and got into the boat, but that night they caught nothing. Early in the morning, Jesus stood on the shore, but the disciples did not realise that it was Jesus. He called out to them, 'Friends, haven't you any fish?' 'No,' they answered. He said, 'Throw your net on the right side of the boat and you will find some.' When they did, they were unable to haul the net in because of the large number of fish. Then the disciple whom Jesus loved said to Peter, 'It is the Lord!' As soon as Simon Peter heard him say, 'It is the Lord,' he wrapped his outer garment around him (for he had taken it off) and jumped into the water. The other disciples followed in the boat, towing the net full of fish, for they were not far from shore, about a hundred yards.* (John 21:1-8)

I want us to take some further direction from this story. I felt

*Prepare to Go Fishing*

God say it was time to again engage in the mission with all our hearts. That it's time to fish again! It's interesting to me that for Peter and the other disciples, when Jesus was not present, they went back to what they knew... fishing.

But once again, without Jesus they were ineffective. They fished all night in their own strength and caught nothing. When Jesus shows up again and gives direction and the disciples follow His instruction, they get another miraculous catch.

The key to their success in both accounts is that Jesus is the central figure. Mission without Jesus is fruitless. Whereas mission with Jesus at the centre produces a harvest. The point of 'prepare' has been to get our lives in order where Jesus is the centre so that when we go on mission, we are successful.

But notice in this second account after Jesus' resurrection, that He now tells them to fish on the right side of the boat. We don't see that in the passage in Luke, but here in the book of John something is different. Its significance is that it represented how Jesus would sit down at the right hand of the Father and all those who believe in Him will also be appointed to the right side of the throne.

*When the Son of Man comes in His glory, and all the angels with him, He will sit on his glorious throne. All the nations will be gathered before Him, and He will separate the people one from another as a shepherd separates the sheep from the goats. He will put the sheep on His right and the goats on His left.* (Matthew 25:31-33)

It pointed to the destination of the catch. That those we are called to reach are destined to be seated with Christ. They were also set up for fishing on the left so this meant a shift in position, a shift in process, a shift in focus. Perhaps it's also time for us to do this fishing differently than we've done before.

Based on that thought – to reach people we have never reached; we will have to do things we have never done.

As a direct result of this, even though we were back to gathering fully again, we made the decision to start an online service with hosts to connect to people that joined in with us.

This was a 'fish on the right side of the boat' moment for us. To take this opportunity to release the gospel of hope as far as we can and connect it to people's lives. Out of the ashes of Covid 19 we were launching a new ministry online with a faith expectation of changing lives.

To reach people we have never reached before also requires us to present Christ to a world that needs Him wherever we go. It looks like praying for people you know to find Jesus, but also being actually willing to introduce them to Jesus.

Notice in John 21, Peter dives in and swims to Jesus. It's a picture for me of the leader pointing everyone to their pursuit of Jesus, but right behind him the other disciples bring the net full of fish to shore.

They are bringing the catch to the feet of Jesus. That responsibility belongs to all of us. We are called to bring people to Jesus, and I believe God wants us to each take on a new boldness to invite.

Fishing off the right side of the boat is obedient boldness to intentionally reach people and bring them to the feet of Jesus. If each of us were to pray for and invite one person or one family into our lives, our faith and our church, we would collectively see our boat filled with people coming to know Jesus, and we would see many more boats being filled in our future.

For me, the goal is to bring people to Christ. And for that reality Jesus wants access to every one of our lives. The expansion of God's Kingdom will increase as the body of Christ, His church, go out active in our faith. Willing to be uncomfortable and saying yes

*Prepare to Go Fishing*

to telling people about Jesus and loving them with the grace and compassion Jesus showed us.

Maybe you have not had conversations about God or ever invited anyone to your dinner table or to church – maybe this is your season with Christ present at the centre to be bold in obedience and reach out to someone. It certainly starts with praying intentionally for the people in your life.

The world in all its mess and uncertainty is looking for hope and something to anchor their lives to and the only stable person to anchor one's life to is Jesus. The world desperately needs Him. Our job in the midst of turmoil and confusion is not only to offer opinion on the issues of the day – but to point people to Jesus.

**Prayer**
*Lord, we thank you that when you are front and centre in our lives,*
*we can have great confidence of success in the mission of reaching*
*our world with the truth and hope of Jesus.*
*You, Lord, are the answer the world needs.*
*You are the God of healing and reconciliation, hope and promise.*
*Because of you we have a true and certain hope of eternity*
*free from pain and suffering, sickness and injustice.*
*Help us today to again be focused on the mission of the church*
*to reach and influence our world with the truth about Jesus.*
*Recommission us again today to go into all the world and*
*bring people into a full relationship with you, I pray.*

*In Jesus' name,*
*Amen.*

Chapter 10

# Stand Against Giants

Preparing for sharing vision is always an interesting time in a leader's life. For me, I get a general sense of what God is saying months in advance of actually sharing it, and sometimes, like the last few years, almost a year in advance.

The longer the lead in, the greater the emphasis in your heart the vision becomes. It grabs more and more of your attention. It also means vision gets refined over time and begins to grow in revelation.

Whenever I get a sense of what God wants to say to the church in any given year, I get peace because a certainty of direction comes. I know where we are going. Every year, however, as I have said before, I often think to myself, when will the vision ever just be more blessing? Everything you do will grow and be amazing – life will be easy and you will never again have trouble!

If only that was what God placed in my heart...

One of the things I felt God show me that you may remember from an earlier scripture was that we were not to build an Eliab church, but a David church. God spoke to a guy in the Bible called Samuel and said to Samuel, 'Go to the House of Jesse and I will show you which son of Jesse to anoint to be the next King of Israel.'

When Samuel arrives, the boys are all lined up and Samuel notices Eliab who stands out because of how he looks. Surely this is the one!

But God speaks and says to Samuel, 'Do not consider his appearance or his height for I have rejected him. Man looks at the outward appearance, but I look at the heart.'

In fact, God rejected each of Jesse's sons. Then Samuel says to Jesse, 'Is this all of your boys?'

Jesse replies, 'Well no... there is David, but he is the youngest and he is out tending to the family farm, looking after the sheep.'

David, who was not even invited into the room, is in the end the one God tells Samuel he is to anoint as the next king.

David, the youngest, while tending the sheep had shown his potential and heart before the Lord. He was a worshipper, and he was a warrior. He worshipped God and he had learned to defend the sheep against the lion and the bear who came to attack his flock.

I felt God say to me in the journey of 'Prepare', 'Don't build me an Eliab church that only looks good on the outside but build me a David church that is as good at the centre as it is on the exterior.'

There are many things that are designed to distract us from living lives where Christ is at the centre and because of that, the 'Prepare' vision was launched. The big question has to be asked... what was God preparing us for?

'Prepare' in its design, was always leading to what I want to begin sharing with you now.

I felt God was preparing His church to 'Stand'. That the world needs His people to stand up, speak up, show up, pray and take action.

That God is preparing His army to stand up and fight because we are in a battle for the souls of the countless people who don't know Jesus. We are in a fight for prodigals – God's kids who have turned their backs on Jesus and/or the church.

'Stand' is a position of readiness for action – it's an active position not a passive posture.

The enemy wants a complacent, passive church that is distracted from the battle at hand. God wants a people who are alert to the times and awake to the situation.

The times we are in are crucial. There are wars everywhere, rumours of wars, pestilence, disease and pandemics, confusion. Distortion of truth is at an all-time high.

God wants a church that is alert and ready. Engaged in the mission. I felt God tell me that He is wanting to reposition many people and He wants to reposition His church from a seated position to, at times, a standing position.

Now let me explain this before you assume that the seated position represents laziness, or that I am saying the church is sleepy and idle. I'm not. That's not what I felt God showing me in the refining of the vision. The seated position is an amazing position. It's an incredible posture.

Jesus himself, once He ascended into heaven, sat down at the right-hand side of the Father. It's a position of honour and it represents authority. All authority in heaven and on earth was given to Jesus, so the seated position represents authority. It also represents intercession. Jesus intercedes on our behalf and is an advocate for us.

*Who then is the one who condemns? No one. Christ Jesus who died – more than that, who was raised to life – is at the right hand of God and is also interceding for us.* (Romans 8:34)

It's also our place of destiny, for those who love Jesus and put their faith in Him are destined to sit with Him on the right-hand side of the Father.

*'When the Son of Man comes in His glory, and all the angels with Him, He will sit on his glorious throne. All the nations will be*

> *gathered before Him, and He will separate the people one from another as a shepherd separates the sheep from the goats. He will put the sheep on his right and the goats on His left. 'Then the King will say to those on His right, 'Come, you who are blessed by my Father; take your inheritance, the kingdom prepared for you since the creation of the world.'* (Matthew 25:31-34)

It is the place of peace and rest to know that we are secure in Christ. That Christ has won the victory and all we need to do is rest in that. But there is a truth I felt God give me as I waited on Him. If we fail to understand the times and the fight, we might just make the place of promise, rest and peace, the place of apathy.

We must have times in the seated position, but while there are still people who are in the world that don't know Jesus, we need the church to stand and fight. Not for themselves, but for those who right now don't know Christ.

It's not one position or the other – it's both. However, if we don't understand there is a battle raging in the earth and the church does not stand in that battle, then the place of destiny and promise can become a place of inaction.

One day the fighting will stop, but while we are alive in the earth or while we are waiting for Jesus to return for His bride, we have to fight for all those who are destined for the same position in eternity as us. The bride (the church) has to get out of her wedding dress and into some armour once in a while!

Stand, church of Jesus Christ. Engage in God's mission. There are people who need the church to stand and shine our light in the darkness.

That's why in this season we are pushing to expand. To build buildings and plant campuses. To run discipleship classes and Alpha courses for new believers as well as missional training. We are preparing for the harvest that comes with a church that understands the times and has taken to her feet to engage in the battle to win souls.

God has prepared His church to be repositioned and if we understand that the battle is real, we will be willing to be repositioned. It will take all of us to understand the mission. We need to be willing to be repositioned to help reach people.

We created a new missions course (CoMission), because engagement in the battle begins with understanding. The church that will thrive in the days we are living in is the church that is engaged in mission, not entertained on Sundays. The course was designed to help us grasp God's heart and to have the Holy Spirit refresh our passion for making disciples.

This course, which was written for us by Dr Lorraine Dierck (Thailand missionary and church planter for 40+ years), saw over 200 people in our church sign up and be impacted by God's heart for mission and with understanding about their part to play.

God wants to move you into a battle-ready position. Some of us need to be repositioned from:

- Attending church to serving Christ through the church
- From serving to leading
- From leading others to releasing others
- From receiving to giving
- From asleep to alert
- From sitting to standing

God wants you engaged in the cause of His Kingdom.

Let's look at more from the life of David following on from being anointed to be king. In 1 Samuel 17, we see that David's brothers had been gathered for a battle against the Philistines but David, who simply tends the family farm, is not present.

David's father, Jesse, comes to David and says to him, 'I want you to go to your brothers on the front line and take them some bread and cheese and find out how they are and bring me assurance they are okay.'

David was just the extra in the story. He was the after-thought in his family and was given all the mundane, practical jobs to do.

David arrives to the battleground to find a Philistine named Goliath, a giant warrior of a man, taunting the army of God with his size and voice. Mocking the Israelites day after day.

He finds a timid and intimidated army, afraid of this Goliath. Long story short, David gets upset with this defiant Philistine and he puts his hand up to fight Goliath. To the shock of all those present, he fights and defeats Goliath.

It's an amazing story. The kid whose job it was to deliver bread and cheese defeats Goliath.

However, the Goliath that roared at the army of God in this account in Samuel still roars today. It may not be a physical giant, but it is a spiritual one.

Persecution of the church is on the rise – the anti-church, anti-Christ voice is getting louder across the earth and in our nation. There is a rise in anti-Christ leadership across the planet. The voice that allows every other cause to have a voice but tells the Church of Jesus Christ to shut up and to hide away.

Goliath is still roaring at the army of God. What's our response to be? For many of us, we feel it's not our fight. We just want to deliver bread and cheese. We just want to serve in the background and quietly help others.

I didn't want a fight either, but God is saying to you and me today, 'I have prepared you like I prepared David. You are prepared as a worshipper and a warrior.' You perhaps came to deliver bread and cheese, but you cannot allow the giant to keep roaring and intimidating you or the church.

Here are four keys to having a willingness to stand and fight that are illustrated in David's life:

1. For David, the battle became personal.

He took personal offence and exception to the state of things. He could not stand by anymore. The battle must be personal. It's not just corporate, I take personal responsibility. I will serve, give, pray and worship like it's personal. I will take responsibility for my role in the army of God.

2. David was led by his practical role into a spiritual battle.

The way you practically serve people's needs will have spiritual outcomes.

3. He had personal revelation that God had prepared him for this.

David had already won battles with the lion and the bear while he was shepherding. Your previous battles have prepared you for today's fight.

4. He had a conviction that God was with him.

God had helped him win previous battles and he had no doubt God would be with him in this. The power of God was with him.

God has prepared you to stand and to fight – to let your light shine in the darkness, and it's in the power of the Holy Spirit that you can do it. If the Holy Spirit gets hold of your heart, you will serve like it matters. You'll give finance to the church and back the mission because of understanding not compulsion. You'll sacrifice time and energy because people's eternities are in your heart.

When the church asks for help in areas of service – say YES, it's personal.

When it comes to giving – say YES, it's personal.

When it comes to being asked to lead – say YES, it's personal.

When the church calls us to pray – say YES, it's personal.

The success of the church is not corporate or someone else's job, it's mine and it's personal. When the vision is big or the response required is a bit scary – say YES, it's personal.

When you're unsure, go back to the chair. Go back to the place of promise and destiny and get a fresh eternal perspective. Take it to the Lord in prayer and then stand up again.

We are ready for more. We believe that the 'more' we need to be ready for is more room for people – that we would see revival. That's why it's important that the church can say yes to stand. We are ready for what God wants to do – all of us are 'all in' and armed with our yes.

**Prayer / Prophetic**
*Generals of the faith (those over 60 years):*
*Some are tired and weary. You have prayed for years and even decades and not seen answers. You are battle weary and have taken some knocks. Will you keep fighting? Go a few more rounds – go for even more. This is your year! God is not finished with you in any way, shape or form. When you pray, when you encourage young people, when you declare truth, there is an authority that God is going to release afresh. The enemy has tried to isolate you as a generation and separate you to make you obsolete, but God is saying He will pay for that attempt. Generals will rise up in strong*

*opposition and will position another generation for victory. Keep praying for the times and for a young generation.*

*Business owners / CEOs / employers / people of influence in the marketplace:*
*Respond in your hearts today. There is going to be a greater alignment between your natural work and the advancement of the Kingdom. Your natural work will have spiritual outcomes. If you will engage your heart at a missional level, God will release greater opportunities to you. Greater resource and greater influence. You have not just been positioned to earn well but to influence others. Engage in a greater prayer life – God will open doors of opportunity for salvation through you and your position. God will give innovative and big ideas to generate income for the extension of His Kingdom.*

*Parents / grandparents:*
*We pray that God would grant you the wisdom to navigate your children's lives in the times we are in. Wisdom on what to say and when. Insight on how to pray and a deepening desire to pray. The enemy has attempted to separate generations through misunderstandings resulting in unforgiveness. The greatest weapon in return is repentance. One generation to another, apologise for any wrongdoings and misunderstandings, be humble and lay down your lives for one another. We pray for restoration of relationships and reconciliation of generations. Parents, show your children how to fight with their own faith – raise them up in the house of God and be an example of faith and love. Grandparents, be exhorters and encouragers and lift up the weary arms of parents. Speak life into your grandchildren and cherish them with your prayers of protection.*

Chapter 11
# Stand Against Division

'Stand'. For us as believers, it's the position of victory... Jesus Christ has won the ultimate victory through His death and resurrection. Jesus defeated sin and death, and conquered the grave, smashing the barriers of separation between God and man.

So, when we stand to serve people and to fight for souls, we don't stand and fight *for* victory. We stand and fight *from* victory.

The world wants the church to sit down and be quiet and the enemy wants to turn the place of victory into the slumped seat of defeat. But we will not take a seat and live defeated when Jesus has led His people to be victorious, to overcome, and to be unashamed of our faith in Him.

The call we feel from heaven is that we would stand, not for ourselves but for those in the world who don't know Jesus. But when we stand and say yes to God we are saying yes to the battle... understanding that the enemy is working hard at rendering the church ineffective. This means that there are many things we as individuals and as a church need to overcome.

The enemy has been and is working hard on the earth at elevating the wrong things for people to give their lives to. He doesn't care what it is, as long as it takes people away from the cause of Christ. The enemy fights individuals, generations, God's gathered church, cities and nations but his strategies have not changed throughout the ages.

The enemy works at dividing. He loves to bring division because if he does, he removes the effectiveness of God's people. He divides where possible: families, marriages, churches, denominations, generations, cultures. Anything where there is division speaks of the work of the enemy because our God unifies and brings together families, churches, generations, cultures etc.

Where the people of God live together in unity, God commands a blessing.

*How good and pleasant it is*
*when God's people live together in unity!*
*It is like precious oil poured on the head,*
*running down on the beard,*
*running down on Aaron's beard,*
*down on the collar of his robe.*
*It is as if the dew of Hermon*
*were falling on Mount Zion.*
*For there the Lord bestows His blessing,*
*even life forevermore.* (Psalm 133:1-3)

Unity is a powerful weapon for the advancement of God's Kingdom, when we are moving in the same direction and chasing the right things together. When the church moves together in the same direction, we get momentum.

The enemy knows this truth, which is why he works at dividing because he knows where there are differing plans and ideas, where there are people in uncertainty of what is required or how things should be done, there will be fighting and arguments that make us ineffective.

Vision is really important. Vision in its design is to bring people together in unity around a common goal. This is the trajectory, this is where we are going, this is what's important.

So, the vision of 'Stand' is to bring unity in our hearts that together we want to reach people with the truth of who Jesus is. For that to be effective we need to make it personal and carry the vision as individuals, then we can see real forward-press and territory being taken for God's Kingdom.

*Therefore, if you have any encouragement from being united with Christ, if any comfort from his love, if any common sharing in the Spirit, if any tenderness and compassion, then make my joy complete by being like-minded, having the same love, being one in spirit and of one mind.* (Philippians 2:1-2)

That, for me, is one of the many reasons that being active in a local church is so important and why I feel people should attend church as often as they can. In our human nature we drift away from what's central to our faith, we get distracted easily from what's truly important and the temporal easily replaces the eternal.

Being in church reminds me weekly of what really matters. It keeps me aligned with God's heart and in the world today when we are being bombarded with so many things, we need to keep our mind and spirit in unity with God's heart and His plans.

Here is another giant I believe we must face down today in our own lives and across the world. The desire to promote and honour ourselves. The giant of self! The perceived truth that I am the most important person in the world. That I deserve the best of everything and should be able to have whatever I want. The desire to be special and noticed.

When self is number one, we will do all sorts of things to ensure we stay that way. The rise of social media has seen the increase of self-promotion. I am the product I am selling. This is not a beat-up on social media – I use it. I work at keeping it under control and when it is, it can be a wonderful tool to connect with others.

However, there is a dark side and a counterfeit side which is the subtle shift to consuming people with themselves. The selfie world. The glorifying of self. The drive to be noticed and liked and special, a performance for the approval of others. Social media is only one of the avenues the enemy is using. The enemy wants to blind a generation to the negatives and has cleverly sold people on the drug of self-glorifying.

When self is at the centre, it is very hard to put others first. It forces people to push their faith into the background because its message is not popular and will destroy the image of self in front of the world. Self stops us going all in to stand up and serve God and love people. It's me first and others last.

There is an old Sunday School song that goes, 'J-O-Y, J-O-Y this must surely be, Jesus first and yourself last and others in-between.' The enemy works hard for you to put yourself first, others last and Jesus in-between (if present at all).

In Genesis 11, we see this self-glorifying spirit at work. It's known as the tower of Babel.

*Then they said, 'Come, let us build ourselves a city, with a tower that reaches to the heavens, so that we may make a name for ourselves; otherwise we will be scattered over the face of the whole earth.' (Genesis 11:4)*

Notice the words 'let's make a name for ourselves...' We are in a constant battle against self. If we lose that battle, we will not stand in the mission of reaching people with the truth of who Jesus is because our focus is no longer others, it's self. When self is the mission, we will never be able to get enough edification to satisfy us because self is a horrible idol. It grows in its appetite for more and more personal gratification. It brings our attention to the here and now, the next thing. It means I am building for the temporary and letting go of the eternal.

That's why Jesus at the centre is so vital. His name is the name we glorify, not man's name, not a church name... nothing other than the name of Jesus. When a person gets the glory, in our human weakness we will turn that glory into a tower of self. Pride will take over and instead of looking to lead a people to glorify God, we will lead people toward the glorifying of self. Instead of raising an army to serve God, we will raise a cheerleading squad to edify self.

It happens in life, and it happens in the church when we have been deceived by the enemy into glorifying the wrong things. 'Prepare' was to press reset on that. We will serve Jesus through the church – we are not serving the church itself. We are serving God not a person or organisation. We honour people and we love the church, but we are serving Jesus and glorifying God – no one or nothing else.

When we buy into the lie that we are the brand or we are the product, we can attract fans more than followers and build a cheerleading squad instead of an army who with one mind and spirit are engaged in the mission.

That's why the vision can't be about campuses or buildings or upgrades or staff or anything other than Jesus and His mission. Those things are great and are the provision of God (and the way our expansion has happened shows that it's God who has opened those doors) but it's only God that gets the glory. We are thankful for them and continue to thank God for His incredible provision, but if they somehow become the vision then we have elevated the wrong things.

We can unintentionally communicate that they are the most important things and in the realm of self we evaluate how those things will serve me. But when the vision is Jesus and others, then it has very little to do with self.

If the church spends money on upgrades and buildings and projects and programmes, we are okay because we understand the motive is Jesus and people. Buildings and upgrades and expansion of campuses are all tools to reaching people and glorifying God. They are not insignificant because, as we read in the last chapter, 'man does look at the outward'. That matters and anything we do, we do with excellence with the motive of bringing glory to God. Excellence doesn't necessarily mean extravagance either – it's doing the best we can with what we have. The desire is to be an army (not a cheerleading squad) that lifts up Jesus' name over everything and is undivided in our desire to reach people with the truth of Jesus.

Another major distraction is the rise of the many causes in the world that are important but are not the main thing for God's kids. Good causes are an expression of our heart for people and love for them. We absolutely should engage in transformative projects, but we must make sure that we are still committed to the eternal state of people's lives more than we are to their temporary.

There are things we should fight for because God is a God of justice but again, they need to be vehicles for the good news of Jesus to get to people. That's why we are single-minded in our global cause of supporting unreached and least-reached people groups in the earth, because the biggest injustice is people not having a chance to hear the good news of Jesus.

The world is an unfair place, but the greatest injustice is having the eternal truth and then keeping it hidden. I met with an organisation recently who do amazing things in the world. They wanted us to promote their cause in our church and it was a great cause. It was 2019 and God had spoken to me about Prepare and Jesus at the centre. I asked if this Christian organisation, which was birthed by an evangelist, had success in sharing Christ with people. The answer was, 'We no longer share Jesus or plant churches because we cannot get enough funding if that is part of our work – however, we are a Christian organisation.' This sounded very familiar to Ange's journey with the youth trust if you remember back to the beginning of our 'Prepare' journey. I had to say, 'Sorry, we cannot support it at this time.' I do personally support the merciful aspect of the organisation's work – but as a church we are on a journey of putting Christ front and centre, not removing or hiding Him away so we cannot give mixed messages to our congregation.

There are many good causes and even God-breathed causes that the world is rejecting because Jesus is present. We as a church want to make sure that the cause of Christ is what we are focused on. We have to watch for the subtle removal of the only name that can save anyone.

Jesus is the answer to it all – there can be projects where without Him it feels good, but we are rendered powerless to change anyone's destiny. God wants His bride, the church, to understand the times. The enemy will package things attractively to lure people into the wrong fights. Look for Jesus – if He's not present then that's not our main fight.

The enemy is distracting the church wherever he can. But the fight God is calling you to be a part of, the army He is asking you to join, is a frontline army that is committed to the cause of reaching people who don't know Jesus with the good news of the gospel. It's an army whose leader is Jesus, whose power is the Holy Spirit, whose cause is clearly telling the world about Jesus, not hiding Him away to make people comfortable.

It's an army that is willing to go without and sacrifice for people's eternities. It's full of love for people and is totally committed to making room for more people to be included. It's not small-minded or selfish. You see, there is only so much room in the cheerleading squad but there are never enough soldiers to fight in the cause of the Kingdom.

When that's the case, we will not fight over disagreements but unite in agreement of what truly matters.

Go back to the seat and remember what I have done for you – the promise – the peace – the rest – the victory. Now stand up and go tell others.

**Prayer / Prophetic**
*Young Adults, 18-30:*
*I believe God wants to release a fresh focus to you. A laser-focused vision of the importance of a strong, clear faith that is unashamedly on display for the world to see. A boldness to reveal, not hide your faith. To have a total commitment to Christ and not live with a divided heart. Your greatest desire would be the expansion of God's Kingdom. To be a generation that doesn't count the cost of serving Jesus but counts it an honour.*

*For the singles among you... In 1 Corinthians 7, Paul is giving instruction that it's better to stay single so you can give God your full attention, but he goes on to say if you can't control your desires then you should get married. Paul's not anti-marriage as marriage was in God's plan – but the principle is that people would live in undivided devotion to the Lord. Free from distractions. God's heart for you while you are single is to simply keep going all in for Jesus and trust Him to bring that one into your life. If that doesn't happen, then you are in the incredible position of giving God your constant commitment without distraction.*

*Lord, release a clarity of vision and clear focus on Kingdom outcomes. Father, place a fresh 'yes' in each of their hearts for the* cause of Christ. We take authority over any deception aimed at this generation. We ask for you to release deep understanding and great wisdom on this generation.

High-schoolers:
We believe you are positioned and called to be a revolutionary army. Ushering in a great harvest of young people. Unstoppable in your passion and conviction to serve God. To grab afresh a global perspective of God's heart for the whole world. To carry a devoted faith – unashamed and courageous. Unafraid of persecution and opposition. Not bothered if your message is unpopular.

Lord, release a fresh fire of faith that will never stop burning. Release an uncompromising conviction of love for God and people. Moral strength and a great passion for those who don't know Jesus. A passion that will never run dry, in Jesus' name.

Children:
God loves you kids so much – we know that God has planned for our kids to be alive for this time in history. Therefore, we will not live in fear for this generation but have great faith that they will grow to love Him and serve Him with unwavering faith.

We anoint our children to be completely set apart for you, Lord. Passionate about Your Kingdom, selfless in life and hungry for the right things. We ask for your protection over their lives and that the seeds of faith that have been sown would flourish and grow. We say, 'Yes, Lord,' have your way in our kids. We declare and release a daring boldness to this generation to believe your Word and dream big for God.

Chapter 12

# Stand Against Inadequacy

Stand is a position of readiness for action – it's an active not a passive posture. The enemy wants a complacent, passive church that is distracted from the mission that is at hand. God wants His people to be alert to the times and awake to the situation. God wants a people who are armed with a yes of obedience because they understand the mission is personal.

We understand the enemy wants the place of promise and honour, the place of authority, peace, rest and victory to become the place of apathy. God wants His church to stand.

When we understand the battle is real for people's eternity – we understand we are not fighting against something but for something. On the other side of our obedience lies someone else's salvation.

We have been looking at this series on 'stand' from the life of David. Particularly how David was asked by his father to go to where his brothers were, on the frontlines of the battle with the Philistine army, and he was to deliver bread and cheese to his brothers and return to his dad with a report of how the brothers were doing.

We know the story – David is obedient to his father and heads off to his brothers. When he arrives, David sees this Goliath defying the army of God and taunting them. Now David finds himself in a fight that was not his – he just came to deliver bread and cheese. However, God had prepared him for this day.

See, this young kid named David comes from obscurity to a fight that God had prepared him for. His motives are questioned by his brothers. God loves to use people from places of obscurity – unknown, ordinary people who have even been overlooked in their lives, who God has quietly been preparing while they have been hidden away. Nothing that has happened in private, no battle that has been fought, no unseen struggle, is wasted in God's economy.

David comes from nowhere to a battle that is not his. But he is prepared for this battle. In fact, he is the most prepared. For some of you – you never saw the fight as your own. Someone else can tell them about Jesus. Someone else can serve the poor. Someone else can lead. Someone else can do this or that. And God is saying this battle is personal to you... I have prepared you for this.

God is raising people from obscurity – I thought all I had was bread and cheese... but God is saying, 'I have got you ready.' Be aware as you emerge to serve God and as you make it personal, people will question your motives... like Eliab, David's brother who also questioned his motives.

> *When Eliab, David's oldest brother, heard him speaking with the men, he burned with anger at him and asked, 'Why have you come down here? And with whom did you leave those few sheep in the wilderness? I know how conceited you are and how wicked your heart is; you came down only to watch the battle.'*
> *'Now what have I done?' said David. 'Can't I even speak?'*
> (1 Samuel 17:28-29)

However, we don't allow man's view of our motive to stop us. We cannot manage the judgment of people, but we know our motive is right – it's to honour God and to make sure that people have the chance to encounter Jesus. The Bible says that God weighs our motive. David was called by God and God knew that what motivated David was pure. David loved God with all his heart.

God knows your motive. He knows it is not to make a name for ourselves but shoulder to shoulder we will make Jesus' name famous.

When it's personal, we will stand together and serve on mission side by side with a pure motive and when we do that, we will defeat some giants.

Back to the story of David:

*But David said to Saul, 'Your servant has been keeping his father's sheep. When a lion or a bear came and carried off a sheep from the flock, I went after it, struck it and rescued the sheep from its mouth. When it turned on me, I seized it by its hair, struck it and killed it. Your servant has killed both the lion and the bear; this uncircumcised Philistine will be like one of them, because he has defied the armies of the living God. The Lord who rescued me from the paw of the lion and the paw of the bear will rescue me from the hand of this Philistine.'*

*Saul said to David, 'Go, and the Lord be with you.'*

*Then Saul dressed David in his own tunic. He put a coat of armour on him and a bronze helmet on his head. David fastened on his sword over the tunic and tried walking around, because he was not used to them.*

*'I cannot go in these,' he said to Saul, 'because I am not used to them.' So he took them off. Then he took his staff in his hand, chose five smooth stones from the stream, put them in the pouch of his shepherd's bag and, with his sling in his hand, approached the Philistine.* (1 Samuel 17:34-40)

A few things to notice in this account of the impending battle:

First, David says to King Saul, 'I have been looking after my father's sheep, protecting them from the lion and bear, and anytime one of them came and took a sheep I went after it and struck it, and rescued the sheep from its mouth.'

David himself was involved in a rescue/recover ministry to sheep. That is also our mission – we are involved in a rescue and recovery of God's kids. The enemy wants to devour people, but we are called to rescue and recover as many as possible from a life without Christ.

David is saying to Saul, 'I am prepared for this!'

The second part to notice is that while David was rescuing the sheep, he acknowledges that the Lord had rescued him from harm. God rescues the rescuers. God was with David in the mission of saving sheep. God is with us in the mission of rescuing people.

David was so much more than a delivery boy sent to deliver bread and cheese – he was a worshipper and a warrior, who knew his God was with him.

So, we see Saul agree that David should fight this giant after all, for Saul has had no one else put up their hand for forty days. It was getting a little tiring after this long and his leadership was looking shaky because there seemed to be no plan. Saul's only plan had been to pay someone to fight this Goliath – giving wealth, a tax break and also his daughter to marry. This is how desperate Saul was for someone to fight.

Finally, along comes David, and Saul is out of options. God releases and blesses those who say yes. Saul's process was then to give David his armour to wear. David puts on Saul's armour and tries walking around but he cannot move in it because as a shepherd boy, he is not used to wearing armour. There is something in that for us all. The mission will look different for each of us according to the skills we already possess. David didn't fit another man's armour. You won't fit another person's way of doing things either. God has given you a unique set of skills, talents and personality attributes that you are able to use for the expansion of God's Kingdom.

For David, it was a staff and a sling... that's what David was used to, so that's what David used. He said no to Saul's process. He said no to something that he wasn't trained in and didn't fit him, and he used what God had put in his hands.

What has God put in your hand that He is asking you to use? What have you got that perhaps next to someone else seems insignificant, but when you use it for God's glory and the power of God comes upon it, you will win an incredible battle?

Can you imagine how nervous the Israelite army was when this kid walks past all the soldiers with a stick and a sling? But David knew it's not about the 'what' was in his hands, it's all about the 'who' was with him. God's power on our simple offering defeats a giant. Perhaps it's time for us all to look at what we have in our hands a little differently. If God is with me, the simple act of my yes along with who God has made me can defeat a giant and could impact someone's eternity.

Don't compare someone's armour to your five stones and sling. What do you have in your hand? What is it that God has given you? As a church, we will continue to believe that when we deliver bread and cheese to the community or city that it will have spiritual outcomes. That as we keep Christ front and centre in our lives and ministries, we will see the simple things have a major impact for God's Kingdom.

As our after-school programme gathers community kids – lives, families and generations will get changed.

As our community café gathers for a hot drink, that drink sows a seed of kindness that will impact eternities.

As the breakfast club makes toast at our local school – that piece of toast would lead to an open heart and a conversation that impacts a kid's eternity.

As youth workers go into schools, lives would be blessed, and seeds of hope planted.

As we open the church food pantry and bless someone with a food parcel, that would show the love and mercy of the Saviour.

As we take care of the needs of people, we would show the love of the Father for His world and that compassion would impact families.

As a tech volunteer sits behind a screen and ensures that the message is getting out online every Sunday – it's about more than pushing buttons, it's getting the gospel out that can change someone's eternal state.

When we don't hide who we are when we serve, when we are seen as the church blessing the city – that would be seeds sown of where people can find help and hope through a local church that loves Jesus and all of God's children.

When we give to global and local mission in our faith offering – don't look at your giving as insignificant. When we support the gospel getting out in other nations and lives are being radically transformed, you sowed a seed that brought a spiritual harvest.

When you paint a wall, when you move chairs, when you serve in any capacity in the name of the Lord, all of it is a part of seeing Jesus presented to people.

When you recognise what you have in your hand and say to God, 'you can have it', your bread and cheese can have spiritual outcomes. God wants you to see the natural and normal things you do, not as separate to the mission, but as central.

When you make a meal for a struggling family, when you help someone shift house, when you help people and do it in the name of the Lord, it is a seed sown or a seed watered.

God has given every person natural and spiritual gifts and all of them are for the expansion of His Kingdom. You are the vehicle to get the gospel out to people. Don't despise what you have.

You may have the role of parking cars on a Sunday – one of those cars had a family that was invited to church, but they are

*Stand Against Inadequacy*

incredibly nervous and your friendly smile helped them relax and finding them a car park ensured they did not drive out again. You may think you only welcomed someone with a smile and a handshake but you helped them enter and feel like they belonged and were welcomed. You may have felt you only helped them find a seat, but that helped them to become familiar with what was totally unfamiliar. You may have vacuumed the building or set the heat pumps to the right temperature, or got the lighting or sound just right. You might have just been on setup team, organising the venue. This shows we care; it makes people comfortable, removes distractions and brings glory to God.

You may have only said hello when they sat next to you, but that told them they were accepted and that the church is friendly. You may have only played the guitar, but the presence of God moves in worship, and they felt something in their spirit that felt good. But perhaps they couldn't understand it yet. Someone preached a message that planted a seed in their lives, but it lies in seed form at the moment. Someone got them a coffee and showed hospitality which helped them to feel like they could stay and then someone else asked about their lives – showed interest in them. They felt like people cared about them. Meanwhile, the kids had a great time at the kids' programme. A series of seeds have been sown. On the way home they talk about how nice everyone was and how interesting church was.

They go about their normal lives but on reflection, Sunday had been a highlight. One of the kids asks if they can go again and they all agree it can't hurt to go again. Six months later, that family is baptised and serving God and everyone looks and thinks, 'how cool is that', and what we often fail to see is that our very natural, practical service was all a part of that spiritual outcome.

That's my story... I am at church and saved because of the love and kindness of a collection of people who were unashamed in their love for Jesus but also expressed that in love for me. And I wasn't easy to love at times!

The battle is real and at times it seems impossible when family are not walking with Jesus or answers to prayers have not happened yet. But let's not despise and compare what we have in our hand to someone else's armour.

You are enough. You are good enough. What God has for you far exceeds what you could dream of. The enemy has told you that you are not gifted enough and has caused you to doubt your ability to share Christ with people. He's told you, 'You're no evangelist.' Intimidated you to say or do very little and you have resolved yourself to being ineffective. We break the power of that lie right now; it's a lie of the enemy.

Here's the truth – God will take what you have been convinced to despise about yourself or belittle as ineffective and use it for His glory. That's what He does – use who you are and what you have, and it all contributes to people's transformation.

You may feel you never led anyone to Jesus but don't be blinded to the part you have played in the countless lives you have been a part of transforming. When you give, when you serve, when you help practically, when you say yes to opportunities in the marketplace, it all adds up to changed lives and impacted eternities.

*I planted the seed, Apollos watered it, but God has been making it grow.* (1 Corinthians 3:6)

Sow seeds and water seeds and watch as God makes them grow.

**Prayer**
*Lord, we thank you today that there is no limit to Your power and even the smallest act of kindness, compassion or service can transform lives when You are present.*

*Stand Against Inadequacy*

*It's not by might, it's not by power but by my spirit, says the Lord. Lord, today I pray there would be a fresh revelation of what it is we each carry and how in the hand of an incredible God we can transform people's eternal destiny.*

*Help us to use whatever we have as an open door for Your Spirit to impact lives.*
*Lord, we want to live with no shame of our faith or love for You.*
*Lord, help us to live big, generous open lives that in such practical ways will lead to great spiritual outcomes.*

*Spirit of God, make it personal for each one, I pray.*
*Every part matters.*
*So come Holy Spirit, I pray, and breathe on us afresh.*
*For those who are tired, fill them with refreshing now, I pray.*
*For those who have doubt in their ability, give them a great faith today in your ability to use even the smallest things.*

*Release a fresh fire today to each one of us with a passion to want to see the advancement of the Kingdom of God and the revealing of Jesus to our world.*

*I pray for healing in people's lives – unresolved pain, unforgiveness, bitterness, disappointment.*
*We ask You, Holy Spirit, to bring deep healing and lasting comfort to people today.*
*Set people free now from the pain of their past.*
*You give beauty for ashes and the oil of joy instead of mourning, a garment of praise instead of a spirit of despair.*

*In Jesus' name,*
*Amen*

Chapter 13
# Engage with the Holy Spirit

Our heart for this series 'Engage' had been stirring for a while and in fact as I look back over the last few years among all the wins we have had as a church, and among the frustrations we have felt – God has been leading us to this series.

I am praying and believing for this series to be significant in the life of our church and our families, and you as a reader, as we launch into what God wants to do in our lives.

However, the outcomes of this series are not down to the teaching alone, but your part as God's child to have a responsive heart to the Lord when He speaks to you. Be ready to respond to the Lord in faith.

That really is what's at the heart of this entire series. Our response, our hunger, our pursuit of God beyond the minimum of a Sunday, as a desire of our hearts for our everyday life.

Why is this so important?

I believe many are living simply in a cycle of what is known to them of faith and have possibly become faith-fatigued. It's dry and mundane and for some, the passion for God's Kingdom is at an all-time low. Many are distracted by so much.

We believe that God wants to pour out His spirit and refill and refresh your life. Reignite the fire and passion of faith in Christ. Break free from the routine into something fresh. For others, God wants to rebuild the broken parts of our lives and bring healing.

For others, He wants to rewrite and revise our expectations. To lift our faith for more and break us out of low expectation and a lackluster faith life. And for others, to reconnect again with the redeemer Jesus in a way where our heart's cry again is 'here I am Lord, use me.'

Many of us (in fact, all of us) need a breakthrough of some description. Many need a fresh encounter with the Holy Spirit to see the slippage of joy and faith stop in their lives. To see the leaking of another generation from the church community to be plugged. And many other declines also to end.

In the lead-up to this series, one of the things God said to me was, 'Carl, are you not tired of all the words?' What God was saying is we need to get tired of just words without His power to transform. All talk, no action!

There are so many words in the world today that people's minds are spinning. We need God's power to transform us and to move in our lives, our families, our churches and our world.

As a pastor, I am so aware that people need more than a sermon full of words, but a connection with the person of the Holy Spirit. If the Holy Spirit is not present, then the preaching is just more words and no transformation.

My greatest worry week to week when I hear people say 'great talk today' is that they need more than a great talk because otherwise by the time they reach the carpark, the talk has gone, and lunch is forefront in their minds.

The Holy Spirit has the power to transform lives and it's time for Holy Spirit to have His way in our lives and in our church – because only then can things truly change through a powerful exchange.

In 2019, I was battling a very difficult year due to a major health battle with an aggressive autoimmune condition that was attacking my lungs. This journey was getting more and more

*Engage with the Holy Spirit*

difficult as my lung function was on a rapid decline, to the point of my lungs beginning to suffer irreversible damage.

My cough was so bad that at times I would briefly pass out from coughing fits. In the October of that year, it was getting so bad that David, our Selwyn Campus Pastor, called the church to prayer for my recovery. I received prayer that night and many laid their hands on me believing for the Holy Spirit to heal me.

I went home feeling so encouraged and with renewed faith for a miracle. I felt God speak to me and say, 'Keep pursuing the God of miracles not just the miracle.' So, we did just that and we pursued God for God, not for what He could do for me. As a family, we took communion together every night with dinner and thanked God for the blessings in our life and asked Him to have His way in each of us.

There was no instant miracle, but it was the beginning of an incredible journey where every day and every week I began to feel better. Over the period of the next year, I went back to my specialist every few months for checkups and blew the breathing exam right off the charts. From less than 50% lung capacity where I started, I now blew the test in the athlete's range! And if you could see me right now, you'd know I'm no athlete!

I was in the middle of my progressive miracle. It is now coming up to two years since that prayer night and I am at 95% – the sarcoidosis and its calcified nodules have gone from my lungs but the scar tissue remains. I'm not yet 100% but I am believing for a complete miracle to take place.

Some healing is instantaneous, and others are progressive. I don't care which it is, but Lord have Your way in us and bring us freedom. The journey is as much a testimony as the destination. This experience released in my life a desire to pray for people to be healed. To have the faith for the miraculous beyond just a sermon. To believe for signs and wonders that follow the preaching of the Word.

Word and power – preaching, teaching and the ministry of the Holy Spirit.

It has been a journey of my personal relationship with the Holy Spirit helping me to put aside my human reasoning and concern over feeling foolish if nothing happens. I've found that dignity isn't a fruit of the spirit, anyway!

I'm at a place of complete dissatisfaction with just a good talk or even worse an ordinary talk and no touch of Heaven. So, these chapters are about us being willing to engage with the Holy Spirit. To engage with Heaven and have faith for a fresh move of the Holy Spirit to bring renewal to God's people.

Renew our passion. Renew our convictions. Renew our hunger. Deal with our sin and long-term brokenness. It's time to engage again our responsiveness to God – to drag us out of passivity or routine, out of only an intellectual exchange with God to a vibrant faith-life filled with expectation.

This all sounds wonderful but for it to be possible, we need the power of the person of the Holy Spirit because God is a triune God – Father, Son and Holy Spirit.

George Barna ran a survey in America and gathered the latest statistics for the state of the church in the US. His very trusted survey, his data and metrics had several conclusions. One was that 60% of Americans who regularly attend the Christian church say there is no such thing as the Holy Spirit. That's not just those who attend at Christmas or Easter – it's talking about those who are week-to-week church attenders.

Many only believe the Holy Spirit is a name given to the power and presence of God.

Here's where I want to launch from… because I pose the question, how many Christians in New Zealand either don't believe in the Holy Spirit or would have no understanding about who He is? How many in our church?

*Engage with the Holy Spirit*

It's not God the Father, God the Son and God the Holy Scriptures. It's God the Holy Spirit. I believe many could, if asked, describe God and talk about God the Father and God the Son. But what about God the Holy Spirit?

In some ways, Holy Spirit can be treated a little like the weird uncle! Right? Not sure if we should invite Him to the party, because I'm not quite sure what He might do when He shows up? Anything could happen if Holy Spirit shows up! People could speak a new language, some people laugh hysterically, He could have some people crying uncontrollably, someone else falling over and rolling around like they are drunk... Anything is possible. And boy, that could unsettle the party or mess with the programme. Not sure we can invite Him then! And not sure I can explain Him.

Today, I want us to be reintroduced to the person of the Holy Spirit. Because without Him we cannot have our lives transformed.

J. I. Packer, the evangelical theologian, said:

*Were it not for the work of the Holy Spirit there would be no gospel, no faith, no church, no Christianity in the world at all.*

The Holy Spirit is not just God's power and presence, but a member of the Trinity and we need to rediscover our love for Him and engage again with the person of the Holy Spirit.

We see Holy Spirit present throughout scripture, not just post Jesus' resurrection. In fact, we see him present right at the formation of creation.

*In the beginning God created the heavens and the earth. Now the earth was formless and empty, darkness was over the surface of the deep, and the Spirit of God was hovering over the waters.* (Genesis 1:1-2)

Where there was darkness and formlessness and emptiness, the Holy Spirit brought light and form and filled the void that was empty. God spoke and Holy Spirit *formed*. God spoke and Holy Spirit *filled*. God spoke and Holy Spirit *illuminated* the darkness.

He did that at creation, and He does that in our lives today. He can fill those of us who are empty, bring form and order to the chaos that surrounds us or is within us, and illuminate the darkness in people's lives. God the Holy Spirit takes what is dry or formless or barren and creates life and form. Let that be a reminder for us all of the power of Holy Spirit to transform.

He is the (1) Agent of creation. He is also the (2) Source of illumination and power.

> *While Peter was still speaking these words, the Holy Spirit came on all who heard the message. The circumcised believers who had come with Peter were astonished that the gift of the Holy Spirit had been poured out even on Gentiles.* (Acts 10:44-45)

Peter is preaching and the Holy Spirit falls. He is a very active member of the Godhead. The Bible describes His presence with powerful descriptions – He falls, He rushes, He descends upon.

Now, if you're a Christian today, you are a Christian because the Holy Spirit illuminated the truth around the state of your life. He revealed to you firstly your sin or your need of Jesus, and then He revealed the redemptive power of Jesus Christ. Really, that's the only way any of us came into faith in Christ. It's not because you grew up in a Christian home. You didn't come to faith because you made some sort of decision of your will. You don't come into God's Kingdom simply because of will or because of lineage or any other way.

We each came in because the Holy Spirit opened our eyes to the reality of Jesus. He illuminated the truth because without illumination, the truth we know about Jesus, the Bible says, is foolishness to the world. Or at best a religious form without power.

Because of the illumination of the Holy Spirit, you surrendered and fell upon the mercy of God.

That's why if you ever wonder why we pray for people who don't know Jesus, or for prodigals to come home, it's because we need the Holy Spirit to rush upon them, to descend and illuminate their need of Jesus. Like He did for us. The world needs illumination.

Mums and Dads, listen to me for a moment... Just growing up in a Christian home is not enough. We need our kids and our young people to know the person of the Holy Spirit. If you have older kids who are not following Jesus, keep praying for revelation. We all need to pray for the Holy Spirit to illuminate and reveal to our kids the truth.

A militant discipline structure is not enough. An intellectual argument is not enough, no matter how clever you are. Isolation from the world won't do it. Prayer and the power of the Holy Spirit is what changes everything.

He does not just illuminate for us to find salvation however, but also so we can understand who God is. The Bible tells us that the gospel, the scriptures, are foolishness to the world. The reality is it is foolishness to everybody without the Holy Spirit's help.

*And I will ask the Father, and He will give you another advocate to help you and be with you forever – the Spirit of truth. The world cannot accept Him because it neither sees Him nor knows Him. But you know Him, for He lives with you and will be in you. I will not leave you as orphans; I will come to you.* (John 14:16-18)

If you find you are really struggling with the Bible, it's all locked up and just feels dry, you just don't get it, you're really struggling, you try... you journal even... Listen, it's not just a reading or a study tool – the Holy Spirit illuminates the Word.

The Holy Spirit who will help you and be with you forever, the Spirit of truth illuminates what the world cannot accept – but you can because you know Him. He will live with you and be in you. But if 60% of Americans don't believe in the person of the Holy Spirit then perhaps the Bible is becoming just a good read or even worse, a confusing read. We need the Holy Spirit to illuminate the Word – to reveal truth to us, to give us wisdom, to help us.

You could read the entire Bible cover to cover but if you read it without the help of the Holy Spirit, perhaps you have never really read it. It does not align with how I think or feel... no, it's meant to transform how you think and feel... the Spirit of truth transforms.

*But the Advocate, the Holy Spirit, whom the Father will send in my name, will teach you all things and will remind you of everything I have said to you. Peace I leave with you; my peace I give you. I do not give to you as the world gives. Do not let your hearts be troubled and do not be afraid.* (John 14:26-27)

That scripture describes Holy Spirit as advocate and helper. I wonder if you need the Helper? The Helper who can teach us and remind us of truth in the midst of the challenging times we are all facing? The Helper who can remind us what is really important? Who can give you peace in every situation.

Are you tired of trying hard to live up to the expectations of everyone else? Trying hard to be a better person or a better father, a better mother or a better friend? Is it hard today when you feel it's your job to fix everything and make things better, to be perfect at work and perfect at home? And perfect online, to either pretend away or hide your reality?

Well, Jesus knew how hard it was going to be right now. He

knew it was best He left so the Helper could come, who would be with you in every situation wherever you went.

Holy Spirit is here, and maybe you are desperate for help. We have to let go of the human struggle and striving. If you're tired and dry and have had enough, it's time to open your heart again to the Holy Spirit. He is here as our helper – bringing order to the chaos, bringing form and life out of the formless and lifeless.

I wonder whether we have tried too much in our own strength to do this faith life – serving in our own strength, giving, praying, worshipping, reading the Word. It was never meant to be our human effort alone and I feel that God is saying to His church right now, STOP!

Let it all go and receive Holy Spirit again. Engage with Him – turn away from human effort and ask Holy Spirit to come fill you again. I felt God prompt my heart this week that many have stopped receiving the Holy Spirit's help. Or in our humanness we have just steeled ourselves to soldier on in our own strength. Many have stopped acknowledging Him in their lives and have tried in their own strength to get by.

It's time for the church (and for me, Carl) to declare my need of Holy Spirit's help. Come Holy Spirit and have Your way in us. We all need Him. Whether you acknowledge it or not, that truth does not change.

I felt Holy Spirit reveal to me weeks ago that the enemy was contending with the Holy Spirit for the responsiveness of God's people. 'You don't need to respond. You're okay on your own. Your life is fine as it is. The faith routine is enough.' But it's not. We must respond to our need of the Holy Spirit. Your open heart and response to the person of the Holy Spirit releases the Helper into your life. It uncaps God's presence over your life, and it is a game changer.

I was in a café this week and had bought a bottle of Coke – I went to drink it but absent-mindedly, I had forgotten to remove the cap. I had an instantaneous nudge from the Holy Spirit and God spoke to me out of this slightly embarrassing moment. You've had the living water all along... it's been with you, but you haven't taken the cap off so the Holy Spirit can't quench your thirst and do His restorative work in you!

Once you take the cap off, He comes and refreshes your thirst but accepting Him into your life causes you to thirst and hunger for Him all the more. The Holy Spirit goes from a bottle, to a bucket, to a well that never runs dry. Once you receive the Holy Spirit, you just can't do without Him. We can't live in this world without the Helper.

I'm inviting you to respond today.

No longer will we allow the enemy to rob God's people of response. We can't stay passive in our pursuit of God the Holy Spirit. We need to pursue God and engage with Heaven.

**Prayer**
*Come, Holy Spirit. We declare our desire for You, Holy Spirit.*
*Fill now every person – come and help us.*
*Fill us. Refresh us. Rebuild us. Illuminate truth to us.*
*Fire of God, consume us now with a passion to pursue your*
*presence. Bring healing to our minds, bodies and souls right now.*
*Remove the fear of man and opinions of our responsiveness to you.*
*Remove reason that restricts us and intellectualism*
*that contains us.*
*Release joy to us, faith to us, hope, your love, freedom, identity*
*and fresh revelation.*
*Lord, help us break past our doubt and fully receive You today.*

*In Jesus' name,*
*Amen.*

Chapter 14
# Engage Our Primary Identity

I want to begin this chapter with a text from the Book of Acts:

> *But you will receive power when the Holy Spirit comes on you; and you will be my witnesses in Jerusalem, and in all Judea and Samaria, and to the ends of the earth.* (Acts 1:8)

This passage was the promise that when Jesus returned to heaven, he would send the Holy Spirit, the Helper, to be with you everywhere and to live within you. One of the outcomes of Holy Spirit in us is that we would be witnesses all across the earth. Not only to be a witness with words but our transformation would be a great witness to others. The fruit of the Spirit flowing out of our lives and how we conduct ourselves would be an unmissable witness to others.

When I got saved from the mess that was my life – those closest to me could not deny the transformation they saw. I went from addiction to freedom, anger to peace, rejected to accepted, limited to limitless! After much deliverance, my physical appearance even changed – my eyes literally changed colour, the hardness in my face and expression softened and my 'ready to fight' posture disappeared. Some changes were instantaneous, and some were journeyed over years of prayer and healing from past hurts. Transformation speaks of the Holy Spirit's ability to bring order to the chaos, to fill the void of despair with love and to illuminate a desperate and dark life and bring hope for the future.

You will receive power when the Holy Spirit comes on you.

Wow, what a promise if we will respond to the Holy Spirit. If we will just open our hearts. What was happening at Pentecost in the upper room? They were praying. They were positioned to receive! Prayer puts me in a place of proximity to God and opens my heart to receive from heaven.

This moment of the Holy Spirit being poured out was incredible. This, for the disciples, was the first moment of what we call 'convergence', where heaven touches earth. Heaven and earth are engaged together. And it had happened outside of the tabernacle.

You see, before this moment, the temple in Jerusalem in the place called the holy of holies was the place where convergence happened. The high priest, once a year, could enter the inner room and offer sacrifices on behalf of the nation – entering the very presence of God. Once a year! One person!

But now, thanks to Jesus' death and resurrection, the temple curtain that contained the presence of God was torn in two. Here we see in the Book of Acts this moment of convergence where the Holy Spirit came upon the disciples in power. No longer was the person of the Holy Spirit to be found in the inner room but now found in us. We became the temple of the Holy Spirit.

I don't have to travel to the temple in Jerusalem... where I am right now is a meeting place with God. That's why we can now minister in power wherever we are throughout the whole world. If you have received the Holy Spirit in your life, you have power to be Christ's witness wherever you go. You become a minister of the gospel wherever you go.

This is convergence. Heaven and earth engaged in mission to the outer parts of the earth.

> *Do you not know that your bodies are temples of the Holy Spirit, who is in you, whom you have received from God? You are not your own; you were bought at a price. Therefore honour God with your bodies.* (1 Corinthians 6:19-20)

Do you know this verse? I do. I think we have all heard this verse in the context of 'you better not smoke or drink, do drugs or eat badly, or be sexually immoral, because your body is the temple of the Holy Spirit.' If that's the only context, we can be left feeling guilty for the state of the temple.

Quick disclaimer: we do need to steward and care for our bodies as living temples as the Apostle Paul was teaching in this passage. That's the context most of us have heard that scripture taught, but it's not just about the way we eat or drink or use our bodies. The context is not 'oh boy, you should feel condemned for that cheeseburger...' That's an important stewardship discussion, because when it comes to self-control and sexual purity, there are spiritual and physical consequences. But let's not limit the power of this verse just to that context.

This is also a passage of convergence. Heaven engaged with earth. Holy Spirit living in us to carry His power to the ends of the earth, to our families, to our workplaces... this is a promise that you are a meeting place for people with the presence of God. They don't have to get to a building and have a priest advocate for them. God, the Holy Spirit, has been poured out on us all so that wherever we go Holy Spirit is present. However, if we are going to carry the Holy Spirit's power to people, we are going to need confidence beyond our flesh.

> *The Spirit you received does not make you slaves, so that you live in fear again; rather, the Spirit you received brought about*

*your adoption to sonship. And by Him we cry, 'Abba, Father.'* (Romans 8:15)

This passage is important for us to understand our position as children of God. It is to give us complete confidence in who we are. It's a passage about our primary identity.

We are not to live under a spirit of slavery which has an attachment of fear, but a spirit of adoption – making us children of God, giving us confidence in who we are. The outcome of adoption is intimacy with the Father, where we cry, 'Abba Father'. Holy Spirit confirms your identity as a child of God.

When I was a kid, I would have arguments with other kids – like 'My dad could beat your dad. My dad could body slam the life out of your dad. I will get my dad down here and he will beat up your dad.' That's what this passage is about... Holy Spirit gives us that kind of confidence.

Have you met my Dad? Do you know who my Dad is? Say whatever you like about me... give me beatings... heck, take my life – to die is gain. Have you met my Dad? Do you know what my Dad can do?

When the enemy comes with his lies, like, 'you made that mistake, you're always wrong, you are not good enough, you're so guilty, your sin is too great,' don't forget that Holy Spirit is in your corner.

When you feel like you're between rounds, life is pretty tough and you're taking some beatings, don't forget that Holy Spirit is the coach whispering in your ear, 'You've already won.' Remember who your Dad is, remember your identity, let go of fear.

Now! With that kind of confidence in your identity, you will be my witnesses in Jerusalem, Judea, Samaria and to the ends of the earth. Remember perfect love casts out all fear. What can man do to me? I know the Father intimately and cry 'abba Father...' My claim to victory is that I'm a child of God.

We all have this battle that rages against us – the lies of the enemy we need to overcome. Undoubtedly, we will go some rounds. None of us escape that reality. I'm aware that I have constant battles. I wonder at times if God made a mistake in choosing me. Like, one day I will wake up and everyone will realise that God had made a mistake. Whoops wrong guy, it should have been someone else.

The enemy works on defeating worthiness. He tries to make us live again as orphans, driven by fear of not being enough. I know that's my battle, but I know many of you feel that way about yourselves too. Why? Because that's how the enemy works. He whispers, 'You are not worthy.' That's why we need the Holy Spirit's help because He reminds you that you are worthy because of adoption. The Helper comes and reminds you that you are a child of God.

Remind the devil who your Dad is.

**Prayer**
*Holy Spirit, we thank you that you fill that which is empty or void.*
*Holy Spirit, would you fill every person right now to*
*a place of overflowing.*
*Would you illuminate the darkness for those who feel unworthy.*
*Remind them now, Holy Spirit, of their primary identity*
*as a child of God.*
*Would You cast out all fear and fill us with perfect love.*
*We open our hearts to You again, Holy Spirit –*
*we say have your way in us.*

*In Jesus' name,*
*Amen.*

Chapter 15
# Engage in the Right Fight

We recognise that in the days we live there is a lot of noise and many voices; ideologies, opinions, views, ideas, causes, conspiracies, false prophets, prophets of doom and gloom. Things that were once wrong are now being called right and things that were once right are now being called wrong. Hatred and unrest are on the rise. I feel conflicted between my emotions and my beliefs.

We need the work of the Holy Spirit now more than ever.

The illuminating, revealing work of the Holy Spirit who leads us to truth and delivers us from ourselves and our ever-complicating thought-life and the challenges of today's culture.

Life is confusing and people are in a spin around what is true. Not so much around theology but ideology. When our ideology (what we feel is right) does not fit with our theology or that of our church anymore, we need the Holy Spirit to deliver us from ourselves and illuminate and remind us of Jesus and the work of the cross. To declutter and bring us back to the main thing. It's the Holy Spirit that does that work. Without Him we find that we can so easily drift to arguments and passions for things that are, simply put, not the main issue in our lives.

Holy Spirit keeps us focused on Jesus. Holy Spirit loves to illuminate Jesus – He did that for us at salvation and He does that throughout our lives when we begin to get drawn into other arguments or distracted by life. He delivers us again to the feet of Jesus.

God the Holy Spirit is not an energy or a force, or wind or fire – He is described that way, but Holy Spirit is God. He is not a new age energy; He is a person and we need to know Him and allow His work in our lives.

> *Rejoice always, pray continually, give thanks in all circumstances; for this is God's will for you in Christ Jesus. Do not quench the Spirit. Do not treat prophecies with contempt but test them all; hold on to what is good.* (1 Thessalonians 5:16-21)

The main part of this text I want us to look at is 'do not quench the Spirit'. Did you realise we can shut down Holy Spirit's work? We can quench Him, grieve Him and snuff out His work in our lives and in the church. To quench, simply put, is to say 'no thanks' to the Holy Spirit's illumination in our lives.

However, this passage starts with 'rejoice always, pray continually, give thanks in all circumstances. For this is God's will for us in Christ Jesus.' So how should our lives being marked by the Holy Spirit look like?

In a world that complains always, grumbles continually, argues in all circumstances – our lives should look very different. What is God's will for us? That we would be people who rejoice always, pray continually, are connected to God on all occasions and are overflowing with gratitude.

This will make us appear odd in current times... In a world that is so angry, upset and frustrated we are always thankful, and this is God's will. The antidote to tough seasons is gratitude. This is how the world should see the church. 'Wow, they are full of rejoicing and gratitude, praying continually.' This is not a self-help suggestion – this is God's will for us in Christ Jesus! Self-help sounds like 'find peace by being centred on yourself and allowing yourself to feel what you feel'. No, be centred on Christ, for in Christ we can rejoice, pray and give thanks.

Then the passage says, 'Don't quench the Spirit. Do not treat prophecy with contempt but test them all. Hold on to what is good.' The context to this passage is prophecy. The work of illumination of the Holy Spirit revealing the prophetic.

Paul writes this because there were those in Thessalonica who despised God's people – leaders who were bringing prophecy. The context is that there were a lot of false prophets and false teachers. The people had become frustrated and confused and so began to despise prophecy.

Prophecy is really an umbrella word for things like impressions, dreams, pictures, a gut sense of God saying something, words of knowledge etc. This is not a chapter on prophecy but because this is the context to this passage it's important to understand.

Paul is saying test each prophecy – don't just dismiss them. Because not every impression or picture or gut feeling is God. It needs to be tested. However, some are God speaking – that's why I don't like 'thus sayeth the Lord' when we bring perceived prophecy because we are called to test if it's God. That's why we will often say 'we feel God is saying' because we are not always right.

> *For anyone who speaks in a tongue does not speak to people but to God. Indeed, no one understands them; they utter mysteries by the Spirit. But the one who prophesies speaks to people for their strengthening, encouraging and comfort.* (1 Corinthians 14:2-3)

Prophecy is not just future telling – but it is by design for people's correction, strengthening, encouraging and comfort. Paul is saying put it to the test. Does it correct, strengthen, encourage and comfort, or not?

> *Dear friends, do not believe every spirit, but test the spirits to see whether they are from God, because many false prophets have gone out into the world. This is how you can recognise the Spirit of God: Every spirit that acknowledges that Jesus Christ has come in the flesh is from God, but every spirit that does not acknowledge Jesus is not from God. This is the spirit of the antichrist, which you have heard is coming and even now is already in the world.* (1 John 4:1-3)

This is the litmus test: does the word line up with scripture? Is it biblical? Is it centred on the Word of God? Test the word of the prophet. Scripture helps us to discern a false prophet. So, this is the context, but it is bigger than just prophecy... don't quench the Spirit. The Holy Spirit illuminates and as believers that illumination at times can be confronting.

What He illuminates in us to change, the revealing of truth to bring us freedom... we have the choice to say 'no thanks' or even 'not now'. I will change that later once I have had my fun. We can say 'no thanks' to illumination if it confronts the not-so-good parts of us.

But this season of 'engage' is about saying yes to the Holy Spirit. Illuminate what you need to illuminate, have access to my heart and life. Yes, yes, yes – nòt no, or even wait. Embrace a yes to the person of the Holy Spirit.

Often in our humanness we run from illumination because of fear of the consequences, but Holy Spirit wants to bring us deliverance from the mess of our lives and break us free from destructive patterns.

The Helper wants to help.

As a side note, that same illumination that wants to set people free is the same illumination that led you to salvation. Holy Spirit draws us to Jesus.

C. S. Lewis described the Holy Spirit as the hound of heaven. He pursues and draws us in. Many don't even know how they ended up in church in the first place. I don't (aside from following a pretty girl to whom I'm now married). That's the side story to the main story. I remember being in church singing, 'you have taken me from the miry clay', and bawling my eyes out with no understanding that the Holy Spirit had illuminated in me my need of being saved.

He saves through illumination, but He also sets us free. If we say no, or not yet, we quench the work of the person of the Holy Spirit in our lives to set us free. When we say no, or not yet, we are in truth being disobedient to God.

> *Instead of asking yourself whether you believe or not, ask yourself whether you have this day, done one thing because He said, 'DO IT,' or abstained because He said, 'DO NOT DO IT'. It is simply absurd to say you believe... in Him, if you do not do anything He tells you.* (George MacDonald)

What George is asking is simply, 'Are you obedient to the illumination in your life?' We quench the work of the Holy Spirit when we delay obedience. I'll get around to that one day. I'll serve, give, pray, go to church, get help, change that behaviour one day. Delaying is still disobedience.

For example, we quench the Holy Spirit when He says we should pray but we don't pray. We know its value, we understand the truth of the power of prayer, but we choose not to, or I will but later in life when I have more time.

The way we quench the work of the Spirit in the church is through divisions – starting controversies and conflicts over stupid stuff.

> *I urge you, brothers and sisters, to watch out for those who cause divisions and put obstacles in your way that are contrary to the teaching you have learned. Keep away from them. For such people are not serving our Lord Christ, but their own appetites. By smooth talk and flattery they deceive the minds of naive people. Everyone has heard about your obedience, so I rejoice because of you; but I want you to be wise about what is good, and innocent about what is evil. The God of peace will soon crush Satan under your feet. The grace of our Lord Jesus be with you.* (Romans 16:17-20)

Divisions and pointless arguments that become obstacles for people and distract us from the gospel of Christ become an issue in the church. Paul is saying stay away from divisive, gossipy, slanderous, negative people who want to make secondary issues the main thing.

We want to get to the crushing Satan under our feet part, but we are stuck fighting over unimportant things and Paul is showing us how that quenches the work of the Holy Spirit among us.

> *I gave you milk, not solid food, for you were not yet ready for it. Indeed, you are still not ready. You are still worldly. For since there is jealousy and quarrelling among you, are you not worldly? Are you not acting like mere humans?* (1 Corinthians 3:2-3)

Paul is saying we are allowing our flesh to lead like we did when we were young and impulsive, but we need the person of the Holy Spirit to deliver us from ourselves and our selfish flesh-driven lives and allow the illumination of Christ to bring us back to what's important. We need this because the preaching of the gospel is not always pleasing to people's flesh life. It can be confronting (it should be!) Have you read the Gospels? Jesus confronts a lot of selfish living. That's why we need a yes to the person of the Holy Spirit – obedience beyond feelings. Holy Spirit is the one who gives us the strength to overcome weakness of the flesh, to put aside the quarrels and pointless arguments on secondary issues.

Studies coming out during Covid in America state that a third of people have committed more than ever to their church family through giving, serving and attending and have decided that this church is 'my people'. Another third are not really sure about where home should be yet – they're still sitting on the fence of what they are looking for in a church family. And the final third have just left. They've moved on from their church. Now what's not clear yet, is where that final third have gone.

What seems to be appearing though is that people are looking for a church that aligns with their ideology rather than their theology. In other words, I will look for a church that aligns with what I feel rather than what I believe. Churches that align with the issues I care about rather than the gospel. So, it's no longer whether you preach the truth as much as if you teach on the issues I align with. I find that sad. Can we no longer live in community and disagree about issues while we align on the main thing?

The secondary issues have now become the main issue and Holy Spirit is wanting to illuminate again the main thing and it's the gospel of Christ. It's not our view on climate change, or identity, or sexual preference – it's about Jesus. However, now are we saying we can't be in community anymore if we don't align on secondary issues.

That was not God's plan at all. It is about the church, full of the Holy Spirit, certain that we are all children of God, passionately in pursuit of Jesus, holding up the Word of God as the truth, regardless of all the other things we agree or disagree about.

Think about the first life group (disciples) Jesus put together. He put a zealot who passionately wanted to kill tax collectors, together with a tax collector! We have more that binds us than separates us – the blood of Jesus binds us together regardless of differences and the Holy Spirit illuminates what's important. Holy Spirit shows us we can live together across ideologies if we keep the main thing the main thing.

That's why we don't preach on secondary issues... because it can and does bring division. Let's talk on current issues outside the pulpit. Let's discuss opinions, but let's love each other beyond our differences knowing it's Jesus that brings us together.

This is why we need the Holy Spirit to keep bringing us back to Jesus. Don't be cynical or negative – Paul's saying that when you do this and when you gossip and fight over silly things, you quench the Holy Spirit.

*And if the Spirit of Him who raised Jesus from the dead is living in you, He who raised Christ from the dead will also give life to your mortal bodies because of His Spirit who lives in you.* (Romans 8:11)

This is who we have living in us... the Holy Spirit. The same Spirit that raised Christ from the dead lives in us! So, how do we get stuck in our faith journey? How do we get stuck in sin? We don't have to.

I hear people say, 'I have tried so hard to get out of this sinful cycle,' but you don't have to do that in your own strength. Remember we have the Helper... the same Spirit that raised Christ from the dead lives in you. I'm not saying it will be easy and it can be messy and painful, but we are not alone. We have help.

Notice Paul is saying fan into flame – don't quench. Respond to, hunger after, pray to, worship Him – respond by opening your heart again and again to the Holy Spirit's work in you.

There are two postures here:

1. Quenching the Spirit

Putting off the change. Putting off repentance. Denying the truth. Delaying obedience. Engaging in pointless quarrels. Gossiping. Negative talk. Fighting for secondary issues.

2. Fan into flame

Obedience to what you know the Holy Spirit has illuminated in your life. Receiving from the Holy Spirit. Opening our lives to His work. Obedience to His call. Confession of sin. Maybe it's time to be baptised – to go all in with your faith.

Maybe you know you have been quenching the Holy Spirit's work. He reveals truth as an invitation into something better. He doesn't reveal to leave us stuck.

**Prayer**
*Lord, help us be all the more captivated by Jesus.*
*Holy Spirit, will you deliver people from apathy,*
*from figuring it out on our own, from delayed obedience.*

*Will you give us courage to respond to revelation*
*and obedience right now.*
*For some, it's responding to what God has asked of you,*
*but you have delayed obedience.*
*Holy Spirit, illuminate and convict where we need it*
*and move us to repentance.*
*Forgive us for disobedience.*

*Deliver us from self being centre and highlight Christ*
*afresh to us today.*

*Pressing Reset*

*For those who need to receive baptism of the Holy Spirit,
we ask Holy Spirit that you come now in power and fill your people.*

*In Jesus' name,
Amen*

*Open your heart and invite Him into your life – give Him your invitation right now.*

Chapter 16
# Engage Your Air Support

Being in the midst of Covid lockdowns and isolations, I was considering lockdown from the church's perspective. My conclusion is, although it's not our preference, of all the organisations in the world, the church will be fine. We know that as the church we don't lose because of restrictions, but we can thrive. Even in the most persecuted parts of the world, the most locked down parts of the planet, the church can thrive.

The church is the one organisation who cannot be shut down because of restrictions or imprisonment or any other opposition, because the church is not restricted to a building or a gathering. The church is you and me and we have the Holy Spirit with us and living in us and the church can never be stopped no matter what might happen. It may not be comfortable, but we cannot be shut down.

Ephesians 6 speaks of the Armour of God and reminds us that our fight is not against flesh and blood, but against rulers, against authorities, against powers of this dark world and against spiritual forces of evil in the heavenly realms.

Let's be aware of what it is we are fighting against. Let's remember our weapons of prayer and praise and worship and Word. Let's not engage in low-level fights that achieve very little, but let's elevate our awareness of the real fight we face.

The Holy Spirit will illuminate again our understanding of

the kind of fight we are really in. Our voices and our lives should illuminate Jesus and the hope we have – it should not illuminate our frustrations and fights over less important things.

That's why I feel this series is timely. Every believer needs to have the illuminating work of the Holy Spirit present in our lives in the days we live. The enemy would love to lure God's people into false fights and schoolyard-level arguments – he wants to get us off message, get us off topic, get distracted by the wrong things and become angry and disillusioned.

The message he wants to distract us from is hope in Christ. No other message or opinion. He doesn't care about your opinion because the message that holds true power, is the message of Christ. That's why the Apostle Paul preached Christ and Christ crucified.

Paul said to Timothy, his spiritual son who he loved and raised:

*No one serving as a soldier gets involved in civilian affairs, rather they try to please their commanding officer.* (2 Timothy 2:4)

The Holy Spirit keeps you patient, soft and loving and He keeps you on message. Be aware of the eternal state of things where Jesus has already won, defeating sin and death. He didn't say you couldn't have an opinion on civilian affairs. But He is saying be known for serving Christ and living for Him.

The enemy wants you in a fight that is temporary, earthly or even unimportant. The enemy wants to make God's people feel like they are losing and highlight the losses people feel, highlight the disappointments in life. Whereas the Holy Spirit wants to illuminate Jesus and the victory we already have through Christ.

So, as you survey the state of things – release your weapons; release your praise and worship, release your prayer life – take it deeper. These things connect me to the person of the Holy Spirit.

They connect me to the eternal and bring me back to the main thing whose name is Jesus.

Secondary, earthly and pointless fights erode my hope, exhaust my patience and alter what is truly important in my life. The devil wants you to fight in the dirt, but the Holy Spirit leads us to the true battles in the spiritual realm where we defeat giants, and our lives are a great witness for Christ.

The enemy is releasing some large agenda items into the earth designed to distract God's people from what truly matters. The message of hope in Christ.

There is a lot for people to argue about. I see many arguments from Christians where Jesus never enters the equation. Every problem the world is facing is a sin and brokenness problem and the remedy to that sin and brokenness is hope found in the person of Jesus Christ.

Let the person of the Holy Spirit illuminate Jesus again for us all and what He has accomplished for us upon the cross. The church must stay out of the dirt and find itself seeking heavenly counsel through praise and worship, Word and prayer.

Your fight is not against flesh and blood, it's not against an earthly agenda or an ideology or a person's opinion. It's against spiritual forces of evil in the heavenly realm. The fight is won on your knees in prayer or on your face in total surrender to Christ.

Holy Spirit is saying the lesser the prayer life, the greater the distraction and the lesser the breakthrough. The greater the prayer life, the greater the victory. Prayer elevates me to a place of the eternal, giving me God's perspective.

*I lift up my eyes to the mountains –*
*where does my help come from?*
*My help comes from the Lord,*
*the Maker of heaven and earth.* (Psalm 121:1-2)

Prayer lifts my eyes beyond my temporary earthly discouragement to focus on Jesus. This is the Psalm we felt for this series. Can you see the person of the Holy Spirit present in this verse? Jesus sent the Helper, the Holy Spirit, into the earth to help us. Notice the agent of creation is present. My help comes from the maker of heaven and earth.

It's hard to see the Helper when I'm focused on the dirt.

Here is another great prayer found in Psalm 118:4-7 (NLT):

*In my distress I prayed to the Lord,*
*and the Lord answered me and set me free.*
*The Lord is for me, so I will have no fear.*
*What can mere people do to me?*
*Yes, the Lord is for me; He will help me.*
*I will look in triumph at those who hate me.*

This is what the Holy Spirit does for those who understand that the battle that rages is often internal more than external. Sometimes we like to highlight external darkness (issues, ideologies, fights) because it distracts us from having to face the internal darkness of our own brokenness, which the Holy Spirit comes to illuminate.

The enemy wants to bind people with injustice and fear and load people with bitterness and disappointment, unforgiveness and pain. But in prayer, the Holy Spirit leads us to a place of freedom. A spacious place, free from the bondage that the enemy designed to choke the hope out of us.

The Lord is for me, so I will have no fear. What can people do to me? When I am engaged with the Holy Spirit, what people can do to me loses its power to bring me down. The reality is that people can do all sorts of things to you. They can disagree with you, hate on you, assault you, abuse you, hurt you and reject you. The enemy knows that if he can stop you turning to the Helper, those things left unattended can have lasting damage on a person's soul.

In this Psalm, we see the key is 'in my distress I prayed to the Lord.' That's why the enemy fights us so hard to dull our weapon of prayer. The last verse we read is a key. 'I will look in triumph at those who hate me.' In other words, I will look at the haters in view of eternity and the triumph of my saviour Jesus.

They may persecute me, hate me and reject my message. However, through prayer I will see through the lens of hope I have in Christ, and I'll live from a place of victory and not defeat. This is how we can overcome fear of man, fear of what people might think of me, fear of what people might do to me, the intimidation of the enemy – the illuminating truth that Jesus is for me.

In light of fear of the future, the fear that grips people when persecution looks to be on the horizon and where there is opposition to our message, fear of raising our kids under state legislation, or ever-changing laws, or growing angst towards our faith... Regardless of what comes, remember the Lord is for you in the midst of it all. Look upon it all from the lens of triumph secured for us all in Christ.

Here is another great proclamation for us today, and a truth for many to grasp hold of:

*Then my enemies will turn back
when I call for help.
By this I will know that God is for me.
in God, whose word I praise,
in the Lord, whose word I praise –
in God I trust and am not afraid.
What can man do to me?* (Psalm 56:9-11 NLT)

This series by design was to urgently remind the church of Jesus Christ, we have the Helper. We don't need to face the future in our own strength. When you pray, when you invite Holy Spirit into your life, when you call for help, you will see the enemies turned back.

I've always loved war movies and I don't know about you, but I can recall countless scenes where the 'good guys' were under attack and victory seemed absolutely hopeless and death imminent. The ground troops were under siege, and they would desperately radio for air support which seemed like it was never going to arrive. But boy, when that air support swooped in and brought down fire from the heavens, you saw the enemy retreat! So it is with the Holy Spirit – He is our air support in times of trouble and He helps us overcome the enemy. The Holy Spirit leads us to freedom.

When I was a younger man, I had a problem with not telling the truth, or perhaps embellishing the truth, or hiding the truth. This entered my life at a young age as a protection mechanism. I was afraid of what my father might do or say if he found out the truth. I perceived his response to my actions would be hostile if he found out so I would lie to protect myself.

This then became a pattern of self-protection for me for any perceived adverse reaction. If I felt people would respond negatively to the truth, I would lie. The Holy Spirit illuminated my need of a breakthrough in this area. I got caught in lies and the effect of that hurt people and damaged and eroded trust.

The Holy Spirit revealed truth in me and I took it to the Lord and to people I trusted in confession and repentance. I turned to the Lord in my distress, and He led me to freedom. As I allowed the Holy Spirit to illuminate the dark parts of my life, I gave Him access and I received many breakthroughs.

I have noticed in the days we live we are beginning to lose the power of the word 'sorry'. People don't apologise anymore – they deflect, justify, blame – but don't take ownership for mistakes and won't admit the truth. My breakthrough came because the Holy

Spirit illuminated my brokenness, and the kindness of God led me to a place of repentance.

If the Holy Spirit is setting about revealing your need of a breakthrough, it's to lead you to a greater place of freedom. When we humble ourselves and allow the Holy Spirit to do His work by calling on Him for help, we will see our enemies turn back.

For me, I saw a lying, deceiving spirit leave my life and a new pattern of truth-telling reside in my heart. I saw the spirit of death – my suicidal ideas, broken off me and flee my life. The truth that my life is valuable and planned became my new understanding. I saw addictions broken as the Holy Spirit healed my life over time. My self-medication addictions were turned away.

Your breakthrough could be one turn-around away. In your distress, turn to the Helper. The enemy does not want you to get the help you need. He wants to distract you and cause you to fight in the dirt and fight for the wrong things.

Turn to the Helper. Open your heart. Invite Holy Spirit into your life.

Call in your air support through prayer.

I have seen the enemy turned back in my life. I know like the Psalmist says, 'by this I will know my God is for me'. Wow, what a revelation!

Therefore, we pray for a fresh move of the Holy Spirit in our hearts and in our nation. Holy Spirit will always deliver people to the feet of Jesus – there we find our true hope, the remedy to all that is missing in people's lives.

Our fight is not against flesh and blood but against the spiritual forces of evil in the heavenly realms. The answer is that we turn to the Helper, the Holy Spirit. Watch the enemy turn back in our personal lives and in our nation.

Change and transformation are the business of the Holy Spirit. His power can do that at a personal level and at a global level and that's why we pray for revival fire to burn. Let it burn, Holy Spirit – in us and in our world. That's why I exhort you to increase your prayer life, increase your praise and worship, increase your Word life – let it lift you beyond the daily grind to a greater faith for renewal and revival. Let it lift us to focus on the eternal and not get caught in the schoolyard scraps the enemy wants us in.

I feel God is wanting His kids to open wide their hearts to the person of the Holy Spirit. Let Him illuminate, let Him convict, let Him bring you to freedom.

General William Booth of the Salvation Army sent a message to all those under him:

*The tendency of fire is to go out. Watch the fire on the altar of your heart. Anyone who has tended to a fireplace fire knows that it needs to be stirred up occasionally.*

**Prayer**
*Holy Spirit, we desire both personal renewal*
*as well as a global revival.*
*Would you renew in us a passion for Christ and His mission?*
*Would you renew a right spirit within us?*
*Would you, through the kindness of the Father,*
*lead us to repentance?*
*Would you renew in us our passionate pursuit of Christ for us*
*and for those around us – this will truly have generational impact.*
*Holy Spirit, we ask that you move across this land, New Zealand.*
*Have your way in our nation, deliver our people to the feet of Jesus.*
*We pray that the embers of the revival fire would be fanned into flame.*
*Holy Spirit, blow across our nation.*
*Lord, pour your spirit out.*

*I feel prophetically we must have a passion for revival deposited*

*in our hearts that would lead us to pray like never before.
To get out of the known routine of our faith and lean in
for a great move of the Holy Spirit.*

*Holy Spirit be poured out on us all now.
Refire those who are weary and refresh their faith now
in Jesus' name.
Unleash in us a hunger and a responsive heart in worship,
in serving, in giving, in loving, in sacrifice. Deposit a faith
in each person now, I pray, to believe for revival
and transformation personally and for our nation.
Release to us a laser focus for what truly is our fight,
I pray in Jesus' name.
Release to us a holy discontentment for the status quo.
Stir up fire on the altar of our hearts.
Holy Spirit, have your way in us.*

*In Jesus' name,
Amen.*

Chapter 17
# Engage the Comforter

Engaging with the person of the Holy Spirit is not limited to a Sunday gathering of God's people, but it is for every day. This is to be our posture and difficult seasons remind us that it's vital – that we are intentional in connecting with Holy Spirit daily.

Prayer, praise and worship and the Word are just some ways in which I can connect relationally with Holy Spirit. It is not about religious routine, or a set of rules, it is about relationship with the Helper.

It's natural, like it is with friends, to communicate regularly with God. It's true, isn't it, that friendships deepen as we walk through challenges together, face life's ups and downs together. Friends laugh together and cry together. The more vulnerable we get, the deeper the trust and the deeper the connection of the heart. The more open and transparent we are with those closest to us, the more they know us and the more we feel known.

That's what prayer does. It opens my heart to the person of the Holy Spirit. It builds an intentional relationship with Him. It invites His presence and Christ's purpose into my every day. Prayer invites the Holy Spirit's illumination in my life daily of Christ's agenda and my purpose within it. It keeps my life's priorities in the right order.

The first three chapters of the Engage series were about giving us a reminder or reintroduction to the person of the Holy Spirit.

However, the last chapter and this chapter are like a little interlude in the middle of the series to try and bring a sense of the prophetic.

What is the Holy Spirit wanting to say to the church of Jesus Christ? When we talk about gifts of the spirit, for example – the gift of prophesy is designed to build up and edify the church. To encourage and remind the church to not lose focus or get distracted by everything else that is going on.

In the last chapter, I shared that I felt Holy Spirit wanted the church to be reminded that our fight is not against flesh and blood. It's not against people at all. In fact, it's not against a differing opinion or ideology or someone's differing thoughts on the world. I feel that the Holy Spirit wants His church to really get this... fight where it counts. In the realm of people's eternities. We all know people who don't know Jesus, right? Are we praying for them to find faith in Christ? Are we asking the Holy Spirit to illuminate Jesus for them to come to a realisation of truth of who He is? Does that reality have my attention? Or are we distracted by everything else in life that affects us personally?

I want to say to you that the Holy Spirit is comforter – but that does not mean He will make us comfortable.

In fact, in our troubles and trials and difficulties and sense of injustice, we often pray for a change. That's not wrong, it's right. The question I ask the church is, what is the intention of our prayers? Is it for the Holy Spirit to make us comfortable? To take away the challenges we face as individuals or as the church, or can we accept that He comforts us while we walk through the uncomfortable?

The mission of the expansion of God's Kingdom won't always be comfortable. I remind us that our fight is not against flesh and blood, but against the forces of evil in the heavenly realm. Against deception and the lies of the enemy.

The Holy Spirit wants to illuminate for us again the true mission of God – that none would perish, and while that mission won't always be comfortable, we will be comforted in the midst of it.

The Holy Spirit keeps God's people on course with the mission of Christ in the earth. That's why we must stay engaged with the Holy Spirit through prayer and worship and Word. We so easily get distracted by all the other battles and challenges of life.

For God's people it's a call to keep on track. To not be intimidated by the battle but to have great faith. The Holy Spirit is your Helper; Holy Spirit is the one who gives us courage under fire, who releases calm in the midst of our storm, who gives us peace in our uncertainty.

*Timothy, I thank God for you – the God I serve with a clear conscience, just as my ancestors did. Night and day I constantly remember you in my prayers. I long to see you again, for I remember your tears as we parted. And I will be filled with joy when we are together again.*

*I remember your genuine faith, for you share the faith that first filled your grandmother Lois and your mother, Eunice. And I know that same faith continues strong in you. This is why I remind you to fan into flames the spiritual gift God gave you when I laid my hands on you. For God has not given us a spirit of fear and timidity, but of power, love, and self-discipline.*
(2 Timothy 1:3-7 NLT)

There is so much in here for us to get but I want to grab out a few things for us that I feel to highlight. First off, this is a passage written from a spiritual father to a spiritual son. It's both encouraging and challenging at the same time and both postures of the letter are written in deep love.

Can I just say – you don't have to be a parent in the natural to be a spiritual mum or dad. The role of a spiritual parent is to bring someone deeper into their relationship with Jesus. To help bring out the call of God on their life, to put courage in them and to pray for them and invest godly wisdom in their life.

Also, not every natural parent is a spiritual parent. As part of the body of Christ, we need more of this special relationship to help those who don't have that spiritual inheritance in their family. Who can you commit to helping in this vital role?

As a firsthand recipient of spiritual parents, I know the eternal value of it.

'Night and day,' Paul says, 'I remember you in my prayers, I long to see you again.'

This is a special relationship. This was a Kingdom partnership and Paul the Apostle wants his spiritual son to be equipped to stand strong in his faith. Isn't that every parent's desire for their kids – natural or spiritual?

Paul says, 'I remember your tears as we parted.' Timothy was to say goodbye to his spiritual father and now would lead alone. The Apostle Paul would put the mission of Christ ahead of his own preferences. I have no doubt his preference (or certainly Timothy's) was to have his spiritual father stay and to minister together – that was far more comfortable.

Then we see in the beginning of this letter Paul writes to Timothy's about his amazing, godly lineage.

'I know the faith that first filled your grandmother and then your mother now is strong in you.'

Timothy is a young man with a strong faith, with great Christian heritage and godly lineage – however, Paul is indicating that godliness alone is not enough. Paul then begins to address Timothy's tendency to be timid. Timidity would hold Timothy back from his ministry duties and short-change his gift. Paul is addressing this with Timothy, and I feel that the Holy Spirit wants to address this with us regularly as His church. Godliness on its own is not enough. Living by Christian principle is not enough. Being a good person by one's willful choice is not enough. The thought that 'if I am godly then the gifts that God has given me will automatically work.' I don't think that's true.

Timothy was one of the godliest men in the New Testament. Paul bragged about his character to the entire church in Philippians: 'I have no one, nobody who has the character of Timothy.' But he still had to write to Timothy and say, 'fan into flame the gift God gave you.' Don't let fear stop the gift of God from operating in your life.

We, too, can be godly and still be timid when it comes to the mission of God to reach the world. As a young pastor, Timothy faced the task of sharing the gospel, which could be intimidating.

- Is it intimidating in business to share the gospel?
- Is it intimidating to offer prayer when you come across a sick person?
- Is it intimidating to be a witness for Christ in your family or friends or workplace or school?
- Is it intimidating to give a testimony of your salvation?
- Is it intimidating to pray and believe for healing when you have carried sickness for so long?
- Is it intimidating to believe God for a miracle or a breakthrough and risk disappointment?
- Is it intimidating to use your giftings in service of Jesus?
- Is it intimidating to be obedient to the Holy Spirit's leading when there is so much unknown?
- Is it intimidating to raise kids in this generation?
- Is it intimidating to live a fully seen and open faith life in front of your generation with godly values that your friend doesn't care about or agree with?
- Is it intimidating to repent for a sinful lifestyle and turn in humility for forgiveness?

So, Paul says in verse 7, 'for God has not given you a spirit of fear and timidity, but of power, love and self-discipline.' He is saying, come on Timothy, you are timid and fearful. Fear is restricting the application of your faith.

That's what fear and intimidation does, it restricts the application of our faith to lead others to Christ.

Timothy, you're a good person, one of the best, but you are restricted because you are timid. I think many of us at different times can relate to Timothy. As we look at the mission and we then look at ourselves, we feel intimidated by the calling on the church and on our lives. But this is why we have the Helper. Timidity and fear are designed to restrict our faith, but the Holy Spirit is present to give us power to overcome the restrictions of fear that we feel.

Fear and faith are at war within us, but when I engage with the person of the Holy Spirit, I fan into flame the gift of God and the Holy Spirit increases my faith. It also means that perfect love is present in my life and perfect love casts out all fear.

What is our posture? The church in New Zealand and across the world right now? How does the world watching on view our response to the times we are in? Do we look timid and uncertain and fearful of the future, or are we certain and strong and faith-filled in the face of whatever comes our way? If it's the latter then let's stay on track with our message of faith, hope and love and not stray.

The flipside of what Paul is saying in this letter to Timothy is to watch our witness. Paul is saying, 'you have been given power (dynamis) to be a great witness' (Acts 1:8), but it must be expressed in a loving spirit otherwise it can do damage. If we show no self-discipline or self-control, we can damage a person's response to the gospel.

We need to be disciplined with our tongues. Let our voices bring hope into the world through Christ. Let our lives bear witness to faith in how we love people (and I mean all people), without exception. Self-discipline is about living with the needs of others ahead of our own selfish desires. This is a true battle for us all. Selfishness leads to fear – I'm afraid of what I might lose... I might lose my prestige, power, money, influence, time, friends even. True Christian love empowered by the Holy Spirit enables sacrifice for others with no fear of what that cost might be.

The emphasis I felt in writing this is that we need the Holy Spirit in our lives to overcome fear and timidity. My prayer is that the Holy Spirit would refresh and revive our faith. The posture of the church and our individual lives must be one of pursuit of God, responsiveness to the Holy Spirit, on our knees in prayer and on our faces in surrender.

The opening of our hearts to Him leads to the opening of our mouths and lives to share the gospel with others.

The enemy is all about fear and intimidation of God's people but the Holy Spirit deals with and remedies that fear and intimidation with perfect love. That's why I have been exhorting you to open your hearts to the person of the Holy Spirit, to invite Him in.

He illuminates truth.

He is the agent of creation and He forms from the void – that which was void and formless He forms and creates. If you feel void or formless or broken by life, the Holy Spirit can create something beautiful.

He strengthens – He is the Helper here to strengthen you for your everyday battles. He has assured you are a child of God as your primary identity – that's who you are, a child of God, so you can remind the devil, when he tries to intimidate you, who your Dad is.

Holy Spirit keeps you focused on Jesus in the middle of all the distractions and helps us keep the main thing the main thing. I felt in my heart that the church needs to be more focused on what is happening *through* us than what is happening *to* us. He reminds us of where our true fight lies and not to get entangled in secondary and less important things.

He illuminates the gift of salvation and the eternal things we have that we can be grateful for when we are finding life tough. He gently and kindly reveals our sin and bondage and leads us to freedom.

I felt the Holy Spirit prompt my heart that the more repentant we are, the more full of grace we become. The less repentant the more judgmental. When we are repentant, we are accessing the cross and understand the power of Christ's death and resurrection and in doing so recognise our own need of grace. When we do that, we give grace to others more easily. When we fail to see our own need of forgiveness, we tend to judge others more severely.

Church, we don't get stuck when we say yes to the Holy Spirit's work in our lives. In our distress we turn to the Lord in prayer and He sets us free. He reminds us that we are triumphant in Christ and when we call for help our enemies are turned back. He is our air support when we feel up against it and the battle is overwhelming. He comforts us while we walk through the uncomfortable and He always delivers us back to the feet of Jesus.

So why should we be afraid? We will not let intimidation or fear hold us back anymore. We will open our hearts continually to Holy Spirit and give Him access to our lives and invite Him into everything we do, and everything we face. We won't fear any loss. If He wants our time, our title, our money, our service, our business – whatever it is He wants, our response is 'have your way.'

Let Him in! Have you truly opened your heart to the Holy Spirit? This series is not about words; it's about a person. The Holy Spirit. It's about Him having access to our lives and everything in them.

So, I want us to pray right where you are – let this be your prayer. Take the lid off and invite His presence in. Take a moment now and you pray, you invite, you ask for His help, you present your requests to Him with an open heart. You ask Him in faith for a miracle.

**Prayer**
*Holy Spirit, we say yes to You.*
*We open our hearts again today giving You access to our lives.*
*Have Your way in us.*
*Illuminate truth, strengthen us, renew and refresh us –*
*fan into flame our gifts and our passion for the expansion*
*of God's Kingdom.*
*Comfort us and lift our eyes to see Jesus.*

*Remind us of the victory we have secured in Christ –*
*increase our faith and cast out all fear, I pray in Jesus' name.*
*We declare that all fear and intimidation would go right now*
*in Jesus' name.*

*We are weary and tired and feel battered around –*
*Holy Spirit, we ask for refreshing and healing to come to those*
*who have been knocked around by life and by disappointments.*
*To those who feel their faith is fatigued or dry, I pray for refreshing*
*and that springs of living water would begin to flow again*
*in Jesus' name.*

*For those who are worried or anxious, I thank you now*
*for your peace in the midst of uncertainty.*
*Lord, for those who have a storm raging against them,*
*I thank you now for your calm in the midst of the storm.*

*Holy Spirit, you know every need and every prayer*
*and we simply ask for Your help in our times of distress*
*as we turn to You.*

*In Jesus' name,*
*Amen.*

*Pressing Reset*

*Praise Him on the mountain*
*Praise Him in the valley*
*Praise Him in the storm*
*Praise Him when it's uncertain*
*Praise Him in the loneliness*
*Praise Him in battle*
*Praise Him when it's dry*
*Praise Him when it's difficult*
*Praise Him when you're sad*
*Praise Him when you're full of joy*
*Praise Him because you are fearfully and wonderfully made*
*Praise Him in every season*
*Release your weapon of praise*
*and remember we are triumphant through Christ.*

Chapter 18

# Engage the Gifts

I felt leading into this series that many had found themselves striving for a breakthrough, striving for survival, striving for identity, striving for more in life, striving in all kinds of different ways. Holy Spirit who is our helper during it all is able to bring calm when life is a little out of control. When Holy Spirit is present, peace is present. And we don't need to strive, but to be still and know that the 'I am' God is with us.

Can I say to those who feel fear – I know that's not everyone, but to those who are fearful and anxious about the times we live in – uncertain or disillusioned perhaps with life, Holy Spirit gives us courage in the middle of difficult and challenging times. He reminds us that God is in control regardless of how things look. He has never lost control. God always has more moves in store, and the light of Christ always overcomes darkness.

> *The light shines in the darkness, and the darkness has not overcome it.* (John 1:5)

We are each carriers of that light of the good news of Christ. The light of life, Christ shines through us. This imagery of light and darkness was common in John's day. It represented the power of good and the power of evil. The power of evil cannot overcome the power of good. We know that in Christ, God has won the victory for us all.

Christ overcame death and the grave and conquered sin, cancelling its debt against us. He sent Holy Spirit to live in us and be with us to illuminate Jesus in the darkest of places. While you and I have breath, regardless of what might happen to us, the light of Christ will always shine wherever we are, and we are never without hope.

The darker things get around you, the brighter your light of faith, hope and love for people will stand out and shine. The tougher the times the greater your witness. So, let's not fear the darkness but hold fast to our faith in Christ.

How blessed are we that Jesus sent us the Helper, the Holy Spirit, to be in us and with us. Our response to that is to turn to the Helper, open our hearts to the person of the Holy Spirit and invite Him into every situation and every day. Even the ordinary days... invite His presence. God wants to be involved in your ordinary days.

One of the awesome things about the Holy Spirit being present in our lives is that Holy Spirit equips us to live a godly life on mission and in community. He equips us to be effective in the expansion of God's Kingdom – the rule and reign of Jesus in the earth. And He wants to use you personally in that endeavour.

Nobody misses out on being used effectively by God. Regardless of your background, regardless of your circumstances, your intellect or your abilities, God has a plan for your life which is developed and worked out in relationship with the Holy Spirit. How does this look in practice? What does an equipped life look like? Well, I want us to look at what God has given us through the gifts of the spirit.

I'm really just opening this topic up and starting us off, but I encourage you to study and pray through scripture about this.

Why study and pray? Well, we learn truth, but application comes through illumination and revelation. We need the Holy Spirit's help for the sacred text to come alive – we worship in spirit and in truth.

*For the word of God is alive and powerful. It is sharper than the sharpest two-edged sword, cutting between soul and spirit, between joint and marrow. It exposes our innermost thoughts and desires.* (Hebrews 4:12)

It is alive and powerful, or active – it bears its weight on us. It opens our lives to Jesus and activates change and right desires within us. So, as you read, invite the Holy Spirit to show you truth. Don't wait for the preacher to preach or the writer to write, to learn. You read and you learn.

*Now, dear brothers and sisters, regarding your question about the special abilities the Spirit gives us. I don't want you to misunderstand this. You know that when you were still pagans, you were led astray and swept along in worshiping speechless idols. So I want you to know that no one speaking by the Spirit of God will curse Jesus, and no one can say Jesus is Lord, except by the Holy Spirit.*

*There are different kinds of spiritual gifts, but the same Spirit is the source of them all. There are different kinds of service, but we serve the same Lord. God works in different ways, but it is the same God who does the work in all of us. A spiritual gift is given to each of us so we can help each other. To one person the Spirit gives the ability to give wise advice; to another the same Spirit gives a message of special knowledge. The same Spirit gives great faith to another, and to someone else the one Spirit gives the gift of healing. He gives one person the power to perform miracles,*

> and another the ability to prophesy. He gives someone else the ability to discern whether a message is from the Spirit of God or from another spirit. Still another person is given the ability to speak in unknown languages, while another is given the ability to interpret what is being said. It is the one and only Spirit who distributes all these gifts. He alone decides which gift each person should have. (1 Corinthians 12:1-11)

Now, there are many gifts – here we see nine gifts in this passage. However, if you read Ephesians 4:11 and Romans 2:6-8 and combine those listed gifts you can get up to about 19 gifts of the Spirit. We can take from this that Paul was not necessarily giving us an exhaustive list.

We have miraculous or sign gifts, we have serving gifts and we have five-fold gifts designed to equip God's people and bring us to maturity, helping us to become more like Christ. Apostle, pastor, teacher, evangelist, prophet. All of the gifts given were given with the purpose of building up and strengthening the church and expanding the Kingdom of God on the earth.

We see Paul's teaching here in Corinthians because the people of Corinth had asked this question of Paul about the gifts of the Spirit. Right out of the gate, Paul gives a two-fold explanation to test if somebody is led by the Spirit of God or a different spirit. This is because for the Corinthians, many had come from the worship of idols and pagan gods and had experienced the effects of evil spirits.

So, Paul is saying I want you to be able to discern if someone is filled with the Spirit of God.

> So I want you to know that no one speaking by the Spirit of God will curse Jesus, and no one can say Jesus is Lord, except by the Holy Spirit. (v3)

Again, we see here the illumination of Jesus whenever the believer is filled with the Spirit. The Holy Spirit always makes much of Jesus. So, Paul establishes the foundation for knowing and discerning if someone is filled with the Holy Spirit. When we make much of Jesus, when He is the centre of our lives and we have the Holy Spirit in us, it's the illuminating work of the Spirit to put Jesus on display.

Then Paul begins to explain where the gifts come from and how we receive them. The Holy Spirit is the source of them all. These don't come through an apprenticeship – they are matured by discipleship and mentoring. You can't earn them like a diploma, they are given to us each by the Holy Spirit according to the will of God.

The objective of the gifts is to serve Jesus by blessing people (serving Christ through the church). Every gift is to be used in service of Jesus to bless others and not in service of self. When our gifts are used for anything other than serving Jesus, it is an abuse of the gift.

*A spiritual gift is given to each of us so we can help each other.* (v7)

The gifts were always given to bless each other. Never designed for selfish gain. If we hold our gift back and don't exercise it, don't use it in community to bless someone else, we are neglecting the purpose of the gift. The gifts are given for the good of the church. And the church is God's plan for the expansion of His Kingdom on the earth.

The term for the church used here is *Ecclesia* or the gathered church. In community to bless one another and to build up the church, strengthen the church. This was Paul the Apostle's heart. He was passionate about the gathered church. We are each given different gifts that work together in community to build the church, and the Holy Spirit gives you the desire and the power to do what pleases God. To use your gifts for the benefit of others.

As a pastor who has the privilege of preaching the Word on a regular basis, I have been given an ability to communicate, but that in itself is not enough. I need the help and work of the Holy Spirit. See, good communication can motivate you – I could motivate you to join a serving team with good communication or to give financially to the church but if all you get is motivation it won't sustain you or transform you and after four or five weeks at best it might fizzle out.

However, if the Holy Spirit illuminates the Word and gives you personal revelation, He will transform and sustain you to a place of continuing service.

*Let love be your highest goal! But you should also desire the special abilities the Spirit gives – especially the ability to prophesy.*
(1 Corinthians 14:1)

I love this. After all is said and done, and regardless of all the teaching in the world, let love be your highest goal! But you should also desire the gifts the Spirit gives. Paul is writing this in the context of a church that has become very toxic and unhealthy. It's dysfunctional and immature. You wonder why Paul didn't just shut it down. But Paul loved the church, so he taught and corrected its leaders and people.

Paul is again saying 'desire the gifts' but the context to the rest of chapter 14 is correction. He wants the church to desire the gifts with the right motive. If you are speaking in tongues and edifying yourself in pursuit of a personal experience, but no one can understand you, prophecy is better because it builds up the whole church. People can understand what you are saying. Desire gifts that bless and build up the church.

In today's language, let's not just look for an experience for ourselves but let's desire outcomes that bless the whole church and build up the whole body of Christ. Paul thanks God that he speaks in tongues more than any of the people of Corinth, but that's his devotional life.

*But in a church meeting I would rather speak five understandable words to help others than ten thousand words in an unknown language.* (1 Corinthians 14:19)

Paul's heart was always that God's people would be outward-focused instead of inward-thinking when it comes to the gathering of God's people.

However, Paul is saying this – eagerly desire spiritual gifts, but there is a caution as well that I felt Holy Spirit give me. Don't despise the gift you have been given.

It's so easy to elevate certain gifts over others and this was the situation in Corinth. They were using their gifts for exhibition and not edification. Those with the miraculous gifts or as we would say 'spectacular gifts' thought their gift was more important and special and in doing so belittled other gifts as less important.

I know this temptation is still around today. Honour of a gift is not the same as value – all gifts are of equal value and God has given to each as God saw fit. If we end up wanting only the spectacular gifts, we can diminish or even despise the gifts in our own life. Delight in the gift you have. If it's hospitality – delight in it as your gift opens people's hearts to receive the word of wisdom or prophecy, or to find faith. If it's the gift of mercy – delight in the gift you have, your patient and compassionate disposition enables you to care for those in the greatest need. If it's giving – be generous in every season as your generosity releases the gospel to people and helps to build the church's reach.

Whatever your gift is, delight in it and never lose sight of the fact that your Holy Spirit-given gift is to build up the whole church. We need each other and all the gifts to operate. You are not less important or disqualified because you can't preach like Steven Furtick, you're not lesser than because you can't sing like Brooke Fraser. We should eagerly desire gifts but not allow jealousy of other gifts to cause us to despise the gifts we have.

Perhaps you have hospitality or helps or generosity, but you want to raise someone from the dead. That's like getting a gift as a kid – your parents had picked out the perfect gift for you and when you unwrap it you say, 'Ohhhhh I didn't want the red one, I wanted the blue one.'

God knows exactly what gift you need. There is no elite, professional, special gift than others that should be elevated. We need each other, all of us. The whole body with all its gifts, serving together for the benefit of each other.

**Prayer**

*Holy Spirit, would You right now have Your way in us.*
*We are simply saying, 'Here we are – have access.'*
*Holy Spirit, would you come and fan into flame the gifts of God*
*in our lives just as Paul reminded Timothy to fan into flame*
*the gift of God he had received with the laying on of hands.*

*Equip your people now Holy Spirit, I pray.*
*Please refresh us and realign our focus on the things of Your Kingdom.*
*Would you refire our passion for the gifts You have placed*
*in our lives.*
*If we have become selfish in our gifts, Lord, we say sorry today –*
*sorry for our selfishness.*
*If we have despised our gifts because of jealousy or disappointment*

*Engage the Gifts*

*or because we have felt overlooked, we turn from despising the gift to embracing the gift again with gratitude in our lives.*

*Lord, release and refire the gift of:*

- *Apostleship and that pioneering spirit*
- *Administration – the ability to bring order*
- *Discernment*
- *Encouraging/exhorting*
- *Evangelism (and help us all to desire to do the work of the evangelist)*
- *Faith – the ability to believe you for the accomplishment of what seems impossible in the natural. The ability to trust you to provide the answers when they have not come yet.*
- *Refresh and refire the gift of giving and generosity*
- *Hospitality that opens hearts and brings down barriers*
- *The gift of knowledge*
- *The gift of leadership*
- *Reignite the passion of the shepherd, the pastor*
- *Release the gift of prophecy to all those who desire it today, to build up and encourage*
- *Refresh the teacher gift, Lord, to bring great understanding*
- *Serving and helps be released to us to carry the weight of ministry to the world*
- *Release mercy afresh, Lord, I pray in Jesus' name*
- *Release the gift of wisdom in Jesus' name*
- *Gift of tongues and interpretation of tongues*
- *Release the gift of miracles*
- *The gift of healing*

*And above all else we desire to be people of love to a world that so desperately needs to know the love of the Father for them. Holy Spirit, release a fresh wave of the Father's love over us all.*

*In Jesus' name,
Amen.*

Chapter 19

# Engage in Good News

I wonder how you're coping with all the news reports currently?

As I listened to the news this week, I found myself feeling so incredibly frustrated by what I was reading and hearing! Anyone else finding all the noise just a little tiring? The constant bad news people receive has an impact. It takes its toll when it seems there is nothing positive in the present and the future appears to be so bleak. People's mental health suffers, people's emotions seem to bubble over – fear of the darkening future increases. Hopelessness settles in and takes up residence in people's lives. Discouragement drains the energy out of people and unnatural fatigue replaces passion and excitement in life.

Life can get overwhelming for the best of people as we are thrust into constant change and uncertainty, loss and pain, business stress or staff we have to care for. Can I simply remind you again today to lift our eyes beyond all the negative noise to moments that reset our hearts.

This is important, because not only do you need constant hope, the world around you needs you to carry hope into their lives, too.

Ange had a word from our recent prayer retreat that fits really well here, so I have asked her to share it with you all:

***

*I lift up my eyes to the mountains –*
*where does my help come from?*
*My help comes from the Lord,*
*the Maker of Heaven and earth.* (Psalm 121:1-2)

On a prayer retreat, I had a view of the mountain ranges and I felt the Lord speak to me, reminding me of Psalm 121. Here's what He said to me:

*Mountains are created by major disruptions in the earth. Earthquakes cause the earth to rise up toward the heavens creating the mountains. But then they become objects of majesty. So it is in the earth today.*
   *See, I am doing a new thing.*
   *The major disruptions in the earth, I am forming into a spectacle of wonder and majesty, causing the people to lift their eyes to me and ask, 'Where does my help come from?' I am answering.*
   *This mountain is unattainable by human efforts. No climber will have victory on it to plant his flag, but atop the mountain, the cross of Jesus Christ is displayed – the ultimate victory that brings the help the world needs.*

Following our prayer retreat, I came across an article headline: 'The earth isn't as bright as it once was.' Researchers have noticed that the earth's reflectance has been dimming at a noticeable pace for years.

How interesting when we are told in the Bible, 'the world will get darker', and here we having science prove that this is in fact the case. I felt the Lord speak to me out of that and say, 'Don't focus on the darkness increasing but focus on "the light will increase all the more",' and that the light is in us.

*Arise, shine, for your light has come,*
*and the glory of the Lord rises upon YOU.*
*See, darkness covers the earth*
*and thick darkness is over the peoples,*
*but the Lord rises upon YOU*
*and His glory appears over YOU.*
*Nations will come to YOUR light,*
*and kings to the brightness of YOUR dawn.* (Isaiah 60:1-3)

This was such an encouragement to me – the Lord is saying, 'I am in this, I will provide that incredible spectacle and the moving of the Holy Spirit,' and people will see that the Lord is in control. We need to focus, not on the darkness, but on the light that is within us and how we increase the reflection of light in our world.

\*\*\*

How blessed are we that we have help and we know the Helper? That does not mean He will take away our circumstances but help us to endure our circumstances.

Holy Spirit releases the hope we have in Christ to us in every season of life. Holy Spirit gives us the strength to endure under hardship and keep our hearts right. Holy Spirit helps us to keep a right perspective on what is truly important in our lives. No amount of bad news can overtake the good news we have in Christ.

But if we don't engage Holy Spirit in prayer on a daily basis, it's like saying to God, 'I'm okay as I am. I don't need Your help.' If we are not careful, that forms a pattern of distance from God. Jesus knew we needed the Helper, Holy Spirit, and it's our prayer life that engages Him in our every day.

Let me try and illustrate it this way. If you only gave your body food or water once a week, you would be dehydrated or in a state of malnutrition. Some of you are in good physical shape but could your spiritual life be starving and thirsty and perhaps in not such great shape?

> *For physical training is of some value, but godliness has value for all things, holding promise for both the present life and the life to come. This is a trustworthy saying that deserves full acceptance. That is why we labour and strive, because we have put our hope in the living God, who is the Saviour of all people, and especially of those who believe.* (1 Timothy 4:8-10)

Paul goes on to teach Timothy to set an example for the believers in speech, conduct, love, faith, and purity. This requires the Holy Spirit's help. It's not achievable in one's own strength. We stunt our own growth when we only engage with God once a week.

Pray if you can for five minutes a day. Read a verse of scripture. Form some patterns. Choose the car or the shower, something you know you do every day, and make it a place of talking to God and inviting Holy Spirit into your day.

If you will do that, watch your survival strength increase. Your ability to overcome the daily grind and the challenges that come with it will improve. Prayer is an invitation to Holy Spirit in your life. It's the open-door policy of your heart. If I don't pray, it's like boasting before God that 'I've got this. You're not needed here. You're not needed in my family. You're not needed in my workplace, you're not needed in my heart.' But really... have we got this? Do you have the answers in yourself? I know I don't! I need the Holy Spirit. Ask my team when I had an outburst this week if I don't need to pray. Ask my wife or those closest to me if they feel confident that I've got this without the Holy Spirit? None of them would follow or lead with me if it was in my own strength.

We don't have this... God's the one who has got this. The world is in the palm of His hands. Trust me, we need the Holy Spirit in every situation. Your spirit, like mine, needs more than a Sunday meal, it needs a daily refuel and connection to the source of wisdom, courage and strength. The Helper is here to help and feed your life every day.

Holy Spirit wants you to not just survive but to be a carrier of the hope you have in Christ to the world. You just won't do it without the Holy Spirit. You could be the most gifted person but without the Holy Spirit our carry of hope to the world will at best be empty or religious.

God wants us in these times to be light bearers and hope carriers. That's why, as children of God, we need to lift our heads above the noise of this world. I'm not saying we should be ignorant of what's happening but look beyond it all to bring alternative news and a different vision to the people of the world. People without hope cannot see a future where things are better. There is no vision for a better day.

*Where there is no revelation, people cast off restraint;*
*but blessed is the one who heeds wisdom's instruction.*
(Proverbs 29:18)

In Hebrew, this proverb was a picture of a woman's hair that had come out of its covering and was blowing everywhere in the wind – it became out of control and was not constrained. It was directionless.

When people are unclear about truth and there is no anchor to hold them to hope, they become directionless. They lose control and hope fades.

The Holy Spirit illuminates, brings revelation and reveals Jesus which gives us great hope beyond the here and now. We know our future and ultimately our eternal destination. However, many don't, and they need you to bring hope to them, bring peace and calm into their situation, carry revelation and another news story – the good news of the gospel.

This is another reason your prayer life and engagement with Holy Spirit matters so much. He wants to work through you to reach people in your life. Let's think back over this week to our conversations and consider what we have said – did we bring life and hope into situations?

I'm not saying we shouldn't have a rant with those we love and trust and who know us about how terrible things are. Of course, we do... fill your boots! However, in conversations with people who don't know Jesus, we should have a different narrative and alternative story to talk about. We have faith, hope and love, we have encouragement and strength to bring to their lives.

How does that look? As we have begun touching on a few of the spiritual gifts that Paul the Apostle outlined in scripture for us, I want to speak to a situation that happened recently as an example of why staying close to the Holy Spirit is the most important thing for followers of Jesus.

Now I have been given gifts according to God's will, but I certainly haven't been given all the gifts as we know that's not how God has planned it. We are a part of a body of people and we each use the gifts God has given us. We need each other (no superstars in our church).

One of the gifts I don't regularly have is the gift of words of knowledge. The gift of knowledge is where God releases knowledge to you that you had no prior truth about or revelation of. Insight into something you had no understanding of. It's pretty cool. I don't have this gift operating regularly but at times God has released that gift to me for someone else's benefit.

God needed me to have a word of knowledge and so in a pretty incredible moment I received one – I'll get to that story a little later. This is why I say we need to stay attuned to the Holy Spirit, so we are ready for whenever God wants to do something out of the ordinary in our lives.

In 1 Corinthians 12 where we read through a list of spiritual gifts, verse 6 says God works in different ways. God can do what He likes when He likes and release whatever gift He likes in any situation when the situation requires it.

God is not limited to a formula. He is sovereign and in control and I love how Holy Spirit releases to us what we need or what He needs in the situations we face.

When I was about to become the lead pastor in 2016, my greatest fear (beyond the fact that the whole thing was terrifying) was that I had no vision for the church. I desperately needed vision and I was praying in the weeks leading up to taking over from Paul and Jill who had led with such incredible vision, God please give me something! But alas, nothing.

On the day of handover, we received prayer and I was believing that this would be the moment, but no, still nothing.

Then that following week as I was walking and praying, I received vision in my heart from God. I was praying when I felt Holy Spirit begin to stir a vision within me and then that began to bring a different battle of overcoming insecurity to fulfil what God was calling me to.

I needed Holy Spirit *for* the vision, and I needed Holy Spirit to *fulfil* the vision.

Here's the point. God gave me vision when I needed it, not just for the sake of giving me vision. I hadn't needed a lead pastor vision before I was the lead pastor. Up until we took over, our calling was to serve the current vision. God released to me what I needed when I needed it. I believe if we will stay walking with Holy Spirit, daily aware of him, inviting him into our circumstances, He will equip us in moments for what we need.

God can give you what you need in a moment. I have had moments where I have needed God to give me the gift of faith to believe beyond what my natural eyes can see. God can release to you the gift of faith to witness or to pray for someone in a moment. However, for that to happen we need to be open and available to the Holy Spirit who is open and available to us. The Helper is here to help at any moment we allow Him.

As I look back on my leadership in the last several years, all the best parts have been the Holy Spirit-led parts. The moments of wisdom, the moments of faith, the moments of discernment, the moments of breakthrough, the moments of healing, the moments of vision... they have all been Him.

If that's true for all of us, why wouldn't we invite Him into our everyday? It takes the pressure of performance off us; it takes the striving in our own strength off us.

Then there are certain gifts that have been wired into us by the Holy Spirit that come naturally and come daily. I have gifts that are God-given that I lean on daily, and you will have those gifts as well. But the times when God releases something new to you in a moment are so cool, something unexpected for a situation really builds your faith.

So, back to my story of the word of knowledge.

We were selling something of my son Caleb's on TradeMe. I had not been involved in this process at all but on a Saturday a few weeks ago I was mowing the lawns and Ange asked me to keep an eye out for a family that had bought this item and was coming to pick it up.

As I always do while mowing the lawns, I was just praying about Sunday's service and worshipping God, when clear as day, I felt God gave me a word of knowledge that we had to give this item to the family and not charge them for it. I had a sense that it was important to give it as a gift. How did I know this was God? Because

I tried to shake it off as silly. I didn't know anything about this family, and this is not how TradeMe works. Yet, the longer time went on, the more I realised I couldn't let it go until I submitted to God and said yes.

So, I went to Ange and told her what I felt and her answer was amazing as always... If it's God, then let's do it. Ange contacted the family via text and let them know our story. She said we are pastors and that I had been praying and felt God had asked us to gift the item to them.

The response we got was so cool. It turned out that us gifting it to them was the right thing. They had wanted this secondhand gift for their son's 10th birthday, but circumstances had made it difficult for them. Here's the cool part – instead of this being a gift from a mum and dad, it became a gift from God to a 10-year-old boy.

The text reply we received was humbling and special. They said, 'we gave our son this gift and told him it was from God for him.' In their text, the boy said it was his best birthday ever, because God had given him a present.

That 10-year-old boy's story and his family's story was that God gave him a gift that he longed for because God loves him. God cares about a 10-year-old boy and his future, and He used me while praying and mowing the lawns with a word of knowledge in a moment to make sure He could show love to this little boy through a pair of shoes!

I now pray that the natural gift given to that boy will lead him to the greatest gift of salvation.

Church, God is moving in the world every day and every moment through His church – you and me. God can give gifts how and when He wants, but He needs a people who are open and responsive to Him. Not so distracted and busy in the mess and noise of the world that we lose sight of God in the midst of it all.

Let's be people who stay open and attentive to Holy Spirit and ready for Him to help us (and others through our lives) in every situation.

You need Him. I need Him. Let's keep reaching out for Him, let's be hungry, let's be persistent and consistent in our desire for Him to move sovereignly and personally through our lives.

Don't be afraid of Holy Spirit. Don't hang back or hide from Him. You hear me say He illuminates and perhaps you are afraid of His illumination. Don't be. His primary role is not to illuminate your sin and brokenness and mess. His primary work for you as a child of God is not to highlight your sin but point you to His righteousness in you. To bring you back to the finished work of the cross and remind you of the righteousness of Christ that has been given to you.

There is therefore no condemnation for those who are in Christ Jesus. He reminds you of your righteousness. If He illuminates sin, it's to bring you freedom. Shame, guilt and condemnation are the work of a different spirit. The Holy Spirit makes much of Jesus and it has always been about Jesus. Dive in and open your heart.

Instead of a prescribed prayer to follow this chapter, wherever you are, I encourage you to exercise your free will to respond and to pursue Holy Spirit – to make this a moment of surrender and a declaration of your hunger for Him. Go somewhere private and just respond in faith and invite His presence into your life. You can also kneel as an act of surrender if you can and feel led to.

The key is to open our hearts. Worship Him with real hunger and invite Him into your situation today and every day.

Chapter 20
# Engage in Spiritual Maturity

The Engage series began in our church on the Sunday before another lockdown and, at the end of the series, we still were not able to gather without restrictions. We had high hopes and dreams of our altars being filled with responsive people in pursuit of the Holy Spirit. We believed for life transformation and miracles as we 'took the cap off' and allowed the Holy Spirit room to move in our church.

As much as I was disappointed that we were not able to gather freely during Engage all together, this did not lessen my desire for the outcome to be a great hunger to pursue God and engage with Holy Spirit, because the reality of a relationship with the Holy Spirit is that it's a personal decision to engage with Him.

It's a personal decision to open our hearts to the work of the Spirit in our lives. Or to close our hearts to the reality of His work in our lives. That's the beauty of God's work in creating us for relationship with Him – that He gave us each the freedom to choose.

Free will. You get to decide and choose for yourself the outcomes of your faith life. You get to choose to engage or not. You get to choose Jesus and His finished work on the cross or not. You get to choose to pray or not, read the Word, worship, lift your hands, serve or not.

God designed it to be a want to, never a have to. You can choose to live by faith in Christ and to live selflessly, or to live by means of the flesh. The term flesh I just used is translated in one definition as human effort.

> *How foolish can you be? After starting your new lives in the Spirit, why are you now trying to become perfect by your own human effort?* (Galatians 3:3 NLT)

When we read the words 'live by the flesh', often we think of immoral living or arrogant living as flesh living – one of the understandings of the term 'flesh' is to live by human effort. The Bible talks about the battle between the flesh and the spirit. It's talking about the battle between the Spirit's work through my life or my human effort. You get to choose how you live – by the flesh or by the Spirit.

Why is that hard for many of us? Well, we can actually achieve quite a bit on our own. We can even have success by the world's standard in our own efforts.

Some of you are incredibly talented and brilliant and smart and your efforts can achieve a lot for you. When that is the case, it becomes an act of humility and will to live by the Spirit. To allow the Spirit to lead you and guide you and to pursue the outcomes that are present when the Spirit leads.

God wants us to mature spiritually knowing that spiritual maturity leads us to becoming more reliant on God and less dependent on self. Spiritual maturity does not lead us to greater independence, but greater reliance on Holy Spirit.

My spirit, when it is in the driver's seat, recognises my great need of the Holy Spirit's power in my life. When my own efforts are in the driver's seat, it leads to a greater independence and less reliance on Holy Spirit.

I remember a time in my mid 20s in the church being asked to run early morning Bible studies for up to a dozen men who were a part of a drug rehab programme and were attending our Sunday services. Most of them were in the programme as part of their bail conditions.

I don't know how to say this next bit nicely, but these were some intimidating men. I had some interesting moments leading that group. One threatened to bite me because he didn't like what I was saying – my response was not Spirit-led... in all honesty I told him, 'Go ahead and I will bite you back.' Not sure that was a word of wisdom, more like a word of stupidity! If it wasn't for the respect of the others holding him back, I was going to be lunch.

It was raw and the prayers and conversation had some colourful words. There were threats and fights brewing between the men. There was a lot of anger and hatred for the world. One of them even stole my car after running away from the programme and his bail conditions.

To say it was stretching to lead this group of men would be an understatement. My own effort was not going to be enough. My human reason and earthly understanding and wisdom would not cut it. I needed the Holy Spirit. I needed discernment and wisdom to know what to say and what not to say. I needed authority beyond my years and a confidence I didn't have in my own effort. I needed the Holy Spirit.

That's choosing dependence on God and letting go of dependence on self. Of the guys who came through that programme and our Bible study, I saw some miraculous changes. One of those stories was of a guy that seemed earnest in his recovery and pursuit of faith. So that you can picture him, he had facial tattoos, was missing most of his front teeth and he looked pretty rough. One day, he came to church and asked me if he could sing a worship song in front of the church. I went to the senior pastor and asked him. 'What kind of worship song? Do you know what he is singing?'

No, I didn't know, but he assured me it was a song to God. While it was very much out of the norm for a planned service, our senior pastor Paul graciously said yes. This young man got up on the stage with his guitar and proceeded to sing a song about a girl. I think it had the word 'baby' in it several times and no mention of God, but he sang it as a worship song to the Lord and there were tears for many of us. The young man then disappeared off the scene and out of touch with us as he completed his programme and went on to work on fishing boats.

I had the good fortune of running into him several years later and I barely recognised him. He had new teeth, was dressed smartly and he had his daughter with him which hadn't been possible under his earlier state. When he said he had been travelling internationally on the big fishing boats I was concerned for him, knowing the lifestyle that often went with that career. He proudly told me that when the ship docked at port and all the other men went drinking and visiting prostitutes, he would go and find a church and worship. The Holy Spirit had truly transformed his life and it reflected inside and out. Without the Holy Spirit's help, I could never have led him anywhere. And without the Holy Spirit's help, he couldn't have overcome his battles and become the man he had transformed into.

More recently, the opposite was true and confronting. I was in a position where I was capable in the skillset I had – nothing wrong with that, it's good to have some natural skills. My challenge was not just to rely solely on my skills but on what God wanted to do through my life. To remember to invite Holy Spirit to lead and to engage Him in my ordinary routine.

It takes maturity to recognise my need of the Holy Spirit's help and to invite Him to be part of what I can seemingly do without His help. Spiritual maturity is living my life in dependence upon God and not upon self.

*Engage in Spiritual Maturity*

It's an amazing thing as a parent to think that my job is to raise my children to be independent. To one day grow up and leave home and have their own independence. If I can do that, I have done my job. I am raising them to one day leave. What a strange concept.

It then becomes their choice as they mature to involve me in their lives, to ask for help, to choose relationship. That is the reality of our lives with God. He has given us independence and free will – as we mature, we continue to choose relationship. We invite His presence in our lives.

Paul writes to the church in Colossae speaking to growth and maturity, he prays for them:

*So we have not stopped praying for you since we first heard about you. We ask God to give you complete knowledge of His will and to give you spiritual wisdom and understanding. Then the way you live will always honour and please the Lord, and your lives will produce every kind of good fruit. All the while, you will grow as you learn to know God better and better.* (Colossians 1:9-10 NLT)

Paul's heart is for God's people to mature and grow to where their lives and the way they live will always honour and please the Lord and will produce all kinds of good fruit.

I don't know about you, but my life is not always producing good fruit and my way of life does not always honour the Lord. Have I got any friends? Or are we all completely mature and perfect as we are? Our fruitfulness and becoming more like Christ in how we live is the work of the Spirit, not human effort. If it's not the Spirit, then it's not the fruit of the Spirit – it's more likely to be good manners and respect through discipline, and not necessarily a reflection of the heart.

The fruit of what my life produces is a reflection of who I am. Is it a life built on human effort or a life lived and led by the Spirit? You get to choose how you live your life. You can live based on your own effort and produce what your effort can produce. Or you can choose to engage the person of the Holy Spirit in your life and produce through your life what pleases the Lord.

What drives us will determine for us if we are living by the means of the Spirit or by means of the flesh. Am I just trying to be a good person and have a good life? Is that your mission? Have a good career, a good paying job? Good family, raise good kids and get to the end of my life as a good person? The rest of the world wants that, too!

Or am I committed to the mission of others? To the go into all the world and make disciples of all nations. Is my driver the expansion of God's Kingdom? Is it to serve God in obedience, to bring good news to people? Is it to love God's people and to take the gospel to those who don't know Him? Is my objective that my life would be fruitful in the eternal transformation of other lives? Is it to be a part of the body of Christ and the mission of the church to see others find hope in Christ? To be willing to be uncomfortable for the benefit of others around me?

Why does living by the Spirit matter and why does being full of the Holy Spirit matter? Why does this Engage series matter? Does it matter? Why does opening our lives to Him and not resisting His work in our lives matter? Why does choosing to invite the Holy Spirit into our heart matter?

We are going to take a look in the Book of Acts where Jesus is about to ascend into heaven to sit down at the right hand of the Father. He appears to the disciples one last time as He had done from time to time over the previous 40 days post His death and resurrection, where He had talked to them about the Kingdom of God. Jesus was teaching them the importance of the Kingdom of

God, not just about them having a good life. The Kingdom of God and its advancement was the job of the church. That's the apostle's passion and that is to be our passion today. In our own effort, that passion is pretty hard to keep alive. However, the local church is the instrument for the expansion of God's Kingdom on the earth.

> *Once when He was eating with them, He commanded them, 'Do not leave Jerusalem until the Father sends you the gift He promised, as I told you before. John baptised with water, but in just a few days you will be baptised with the Holy Spirit. 'So when the apostles were with Jesus, they kept asking him, 'Lord, has the time come for you to free Israel and restore our kingdom?'*
> 
> *He replied, 'The Father alone has the authority to set those dates and times, and they are not for you to know. But you will receive power when the Holy Spirit comes upon you. And you will be my witnesses, telling people about me everywhere – in Jerusalem, throughout Judea, in Samaria, and to the ends of the earth.'*
> 
> *After saying this, He was taken up into a cloud while they were watching, and they could no longer see Him. As they strained to see Him rising into heaven, two white-robed men suddenly stood among them. 'Men of Galilee,' they said, 'why are you standing here staring into heaven? Jesus has been taken from you into heaven, but some day he will return from heaven in the same way you saw Him go!'* (Acts 1:4-11)

There is so much in here for us. What a moment watching Jesus ascend into heaven! The apostles got a glimpse of what Christ's coming again would be like through witnessing His ascension into heaven. Some day He will return in the same way they saw Him go.

I want you to notice today one of Jesus' final instructions in verse 4:

> *Do not leave Jerusalem until the Father sends you the gift He promised, as I told you before.*

He had spent His time explaining the Kingdom, explaining the mission of the church, but instructs them not to go until the Holy Spirit has come.

> *Do not leave Jerusalem until you have received the gift the Father promised. In a few days you will be baptised in the Holy Spirit.*

If the apostles, who had been taught and trained by Jesus himself in person, needed to wait for the Holy Spirit's baptism to live out the mission of Christ, do you not think today we also need that same baptism?

Our human effort will not get the job done. It's noble, but it lacks power. Do we honestly think that the apostles who birthed the early church, who were equipped with the Holy Spirit and the gifts of the Spirit, that it ended with them? If that were true, then God's plan throughout the rest of history is for the church to strive and struggle in our own strength, under-prepared and ill-equipped for the task of the Great Commission.

Well, we know through the teachings of the Apostle Paul that the gifts of the Spirit were for the church of Jesus Christ. That the Holy Spirit equips us and enables us to live lives on mission.

Let's look at Acts 1, verse 8:

> *But you will receive power when the Holy Spirit comes upon you. And you will be my witnesses, telling people about me everywhere – in Jerusalem, throughout Judea, in Samaria, and to the ends of the earth.*

You will receive power when the Holy Spirit comes upon you.

The result will be that you will be my witnesses everywhere – in Jerusalem where the first encounter and many subsequent encounters with the Holy Spirit happened, then it would spread to Judea and Samaria and to the ends of the earth.

The apostles were never going to make it themselves to every part of the planet, but by the power of the Holy Spirit the church throughout the ages would spread out to the outer parts of the earth to be Christ's witnesses. That includes us today. That wherever we would go, because of the power of the Holy Spirit in our lives, we would be His witnesses wherever we find ourselves. We would not be left to struggle and strive and be forced into human effort only. But the Holy Spirit was poured out on us also so that we would be witnesses.

The first expression we see after the followers of Jesus have encountered the baptism of the Holy Spirit is that Peter preaches and 3000 people are saved. As the community of believers was formed, the Bible tells us that God added to their numbers daily those who were being saved.

Your life and my life's purpose when we gave our lives to Jesus received through the illumination of the Holy Spirit is the mission to go into all the world and make fully devoted followers of Jesus.

This series is about us engaging with the person of the Holy Spirit – it's your choice to open your life to Him. Do you need Him? If your answer to that question is no, then I pray for you that God would lead you to a place that would require you to recognise your need of Him. Like for me, leading that group of men, I could recognise my limitations in my own effort – I pray, too, that you will recognise your own human limitations through effort alone. If your answer was yes – it's the choice of each of us to open our lives and hearts to the person of the Holy Spirit.

Why don't you just take a moment and exercise your free will and choose. Choose to invite the Holy Spirit into your life again. If you have been living in human effort, why don't you choose today to give an invitation to the Holy Spirit – come baptise me, come fill my life – either for the first time or for the hundredth time.

**Prayer**

*Holy Spirit, have Your way in us.*
*For those who have doubts or are uncertain, would You give them*
*a confidence today to open their hearts to You?*
*To let go of human effort and control and let You in.*
*Would You deposit in us a hunger for Your presence in our lives,*
*whether we are stretched or whether we are comfortable,*
*would You place a hunger in our hearts again today?*
*Deposit a deepening desire for the person of the Holy Spirit*
*in our lives.*
*Lord, we are Yours.*
*When we said yes to Jesus we said yes to transformation.*
*That yes was us opening our hearts to relationship*
*not a journey into religion.*
*It was an openness to the God of the universe –*
*Father, Son and Holy Spirit to have Your way in us.*
*So, we simply again today say have Your way in us.*

*In Jesus' name,*
*Amen.*

# Conclusion

Prepare. Stand. Engage. These were three series that were part of God bringing the correct order to our lives and our church. They were to encourage us that our faith had to be our own – we couldn't rely on the faith of a previous generation, the faith of the pastor or the collective faith of the church. We are in a time in history where there are so many voices and opinions, so many fights and arguments, so much noise in general that we have to learn as individuals to draw away and seek God for ourselves.

Jesus must be central in our lives. We need to take responsibility and ownership over the state of our lives – mess and all and do the hard and painful work of addressing and remedying it with God's help. We need to decide in the times we are in, to keep the main thing the main thing and not get distracted by the enemy's strategies to divert our attention to secondary issues. We need to recognise that we are in a fight – not with people but with spiritual forces that seek to bring darkness to every part of our world. We have been given the authority to stand, to fight and to overcome the enemy if we pick up our weapons of prayer, worship and the Word.

We have also been sent a helper – we must invite the Holy Spirit to equip, enable and empower us for every good work with the ultimate desire to reach people for the Kingdom of God. It's our choice to give room and invitation to the Holy Spirit to transform us and breathe on our God-given gifts for the sake of others.

Ultimately, this book and the journey of these three series comes down to one word: *Obedience*.

The simple, yet profound act of giving God your 'yes' to all He asks of you.

I pray that these chapters have brought you encouragement and helped bring a redefined perspective in your faith that would cause you to go 'all in' for the things of the Kingdom.

On the other side of your obedience lies someone else's salvation.

# About the Authors

Carl and Angela Crocker are the Lead Pastors of Life Church in Christchurch, New Zealand. Starting out as youth pastors, they have been on pastoral staff since 2007 and began leading the church in March 2016. Life Church is a multisite church and values being multicultural and intergenerational.

Carl and Angela have been married since 2000 and have two great kids, Caleb and Elise.

You can find out more about Life Church at www.lifechurch.nz

www.ingramcontent.com/pod-product-compliance
Lightning Source LLC
Chambersburg PA
CBHW062047290426
44109CB00027B/2759